CURRICULUM ADMINISTRATION

CURRICULUM

ADMINISTRATION

Principles and Techniques of Curriculum Development

John D. McNeil

ASSOCIATE PROFESSOR OF EDUCATION
University of California at Los Angeles

THE MACMILLAN COMPANY, NEW YORK
COLLIER—MACMILLAN LIMITED, LONDON

74957

JUN 1 9 1967

© Copyright, John D. McNeil, 1965

First Printing

Library of Congress catalog card number: 65–10325

THE MACMILLAN COMPANY, NEW YORK
COLLIER–MACMILLAN CANADA, LTD., TORONTO, ONTARIO

Printed in the United States of America

Preface

THIS BOOK is designed for school board members, school administrators and others who are interested in the study of curriculum. Its purpose is only to lay a foundation for such study, to open up the subject and give the readers necessary tools for working in the field of curricular thought.

Without too much regard to traditional modes, but with an avoidance of eccentricity and intentional novelty, the form and arrangement given to the content of this book reflect a natural approach to the development of an attitude of mind toward curriculum.

Not everything that ought to go into the minds of persons making decisions in curriculum is in the book. Much has been intentionally left to the reader. It is believed that the book is well suited as a textbook in either theory of curriculum or foundations of curriculum development or as a supplement in general introduction to educational administration. School and community leaders will find the parts, chapters, and paragraphs to be useful *texts* in the conduct of discourse upon curriculum for their schools.

JOHN D. MCNEIL

CONTENTS

CURRICULUM ADMINISTRATION

PART I. CURRENT EMPHASIS IN EDUCATION

THE TENDENCY of educational practitioners to react to transient public pressures, to follow for one year or several years this or that new course and method of teaching, and then suddenly to latch onto a different emphasis is possible because those making curricular decisions lack intellectual understanding of what is central in curriculum and instruction.

Currently, we are witnessing a renaissance of three important educational emphases which can become either the basis for improved instruction or passing fads, depending upon the level of understanding of school leaders.

The first emphasis is in demands that the school concern itself with the *ways* pupils learn, as well as with *what* they learn. This concern comes under the rubrics of discovery learning, inquiry training, problem-solving, and the process goals of education. Chapter 1 seeks to equip the reader with information necessary for going beyond the superficial acceptance of discovery learning and to arrival at judicious judgments of proposals calling for its use.

The second emphasis is programed instruction. This development in learning is a return of a didactic form of teaching but a return in a new form, one which capitalizes upon advances in technology of instruction and experimental research. Programed learning (teaching machines) are considered in Chapter 2 in terms of their promise as well as their present state.

The third emphasis is organized knowledge. Today's curricu-

1

lum is associated with a "return to subject matter," the development of understanding of certain disciplines of thought. These disciplines are presumed to equip one for inquiry and explanation in restricted aspects of life. The status of organized knowledge as it is influencing the curriculum and the teaching of disciplines is described in Chapter 3. Explanation of newer course offerings is given, with full recognition of the assumption that the proper way to develop comprehension in and of a field is to treat a few fundamental topics thoroughly so that the principles involved are made clear and then to build on this knowledge by considering ways in which these principles underlie any specific part of the environment with which the discipline deals. Application to the wide problems of daily living of generalizations drawn from various disciplines is diminishing; instead, application of a discipline's generalizations is directed at problems in the restricted environment of special concern to those practicing in the discipline.

I. Discovery Learning

AMONG RECURRING PROBLEMS in curriculum administration are the assessment of teaching and the selection of instructional materials. Currently, many teachers are being categorized and judged on the basis of the degree to which their presentations call for "the act of discovery" as opposed to "telling." Similarly, many publishers are stressing the desirability of their latest textbooks, purporting that newer editions offer content consistent with the prized "learning by discovery."

To serve the reader properly, as he considers decisions which affect the professional life of the teacher and which embrace costly substitutions of instructional materials, this section should clarify the term "discovery" as method and indicate some of its strengths and weaknesses.

Method of Discovery as Inductive Thought

The method of discovery in learning is not new, even though it happens to be receiving emphasis at the moment. As a method of intellectual mastery, it has been variously named in history in accordance with the prominence given the separate steps of its inductive process. Because it frequently begins with actual objects or individual instances, it has been called the *objective* method. Because it requires analysis, it has been called the *analytic* method, and because the method begins with particular instances or examples and through analysis arrives at general propositions, it has been entitled the *inductive* method. A simple illustration of these inductive steps can be seen in an approach to geographical comprehension of a city. A child begins with particulars, concrete parts or elements in the city, e.g., the school, drugstore (objects). Next, he separates these elements according to such characteristics or functions as transportation, residence, manufacturing (analysis). When he can combine and classify new elements of the city in accordance with their common characteristics or functions, we say he has generalized or synthesized his information and knows the city as an aggregate.

The teacher is chiefly concerned with ordering the presentation of elements and with selecting the abstractions or functions which will permit analysis and fruitful generalizations. Left to chance or in the absence of the teacher, a learner is likely to arrive at an inadequate generalization or incorrect synthesis. It is a fact that many children characterize objects according to misleading external features. In differentiating, for example, the concepts "bird" and "insect," some give decisive significance to the feature of flying. This classification does not allow them to class as birds domestic ducks and hens which do not fly; conversely, it makes them classify insects like beetles and butterflies as birds.

Discovery and Non-Discovery Teaching

The degree to which the teacher provides direction during the discovery process has become a source of confusion regarding the meaning of discovery learning. There are those teachers who present a problem and require the learner to "discover" the solution without help during the process. Other teachers present clues to help learners discover the appropriate rules or solutions. We say that both teachers are using a discovery method on the ground that a generalization is deferred until found by the learner. In contrast, a teacher who gives the rules or solution outright and then offers examples for practice is not following a discovery method.

Method of Discovery and Characteristics of Subject Matter

It is logical to assume that the method of discovery is appropriate for the learning of some subject matter and not for other. The essence of science is abstraction proceeding "from the particular to the general." An inductive method is therefore appropriate for scientific inquiry. The natural sciences have been built up from empirical knowledge of mere facts into systematic knowledge consisting of laws and principles through the method of discovery. Therefore, it can be argued that this method is appropriate to use in the teaching of science. On the other hand, art is not concerned with "universal generalizations," but with the unique and particular (e.g., the art object). Also, mathematical studies are usually deductive in nature. Euclidian geometry, for example, starts with axioms and conventional definitions. Its first theorems are of the general character. Out of these are unfolded narrower propositions. History is produced, not through first-hand experience with historical events but with the general judgments of the historian which he brings to bear in interpreting selected aspects of history. Therefore, it might be reasoned that the teaching of nonscientific subjects which have their own noninductive methods of inquiry would be better advanced by different approaches. In fact, however, no science or art completes itself by either the inductive or deductive method alone. There are times when the artist must induce and times when the scientist must deduce. Furthermore, if the teacher in any subject area wants learners to engage in inquiry or to resolve perplexing situations which occur within that field of knowledge, then the teacher must give them the opportunity to practice inquiry and to engage in discovering a solution to such perplexities.

Acquiring versus Inquiring and the Discovery Method

Concern for developing inquiring or searching behavior underlies much of today's emphasis upon discovery learning. This concern is expressed as a popularly held, but misleading, dichotomy. We tend to differentiate acquiring from inquiring. Acquiring is seen as getting and keeping what is known or already discovered. Inquiring is held to be the process of questioning and searching in dealing with the unknown. It follows that at a time when new discoveries are being made at a rapid rate and old discoveries are being discarded or corrected, schools should be asked to stress the process or methods of inquiry rather than conclusions, or the fruits of inquiring. The falseness of the dichotomy lies in the fact that the processes of inquiry to be taught (strategies for learning) are conclusions or previously discovered answers just as much as any other predetermined set of answers, concepts, and generalizations.

When school officials decide that the learner will acquire understanding of the procedures for conducting inquiry in, say, sociology, instead of acquiring information describing social change among a particular group of people, they have made a value judgment about instructional objectives and the kind of knowledge to be taught; they have not departed from a concern for acquisition of knowledge. The "knowledge" has shifted from that which is static to that knowledge which is associated with the dynamics of inquiry.

Searching behavior or procedures for conducting inquiry are not the same as the discovery method. As a matter of fact, there is little established knowledge as to what the prerequisites are for discovering new truths in different fields. The great range of assumed prerequisites for inquiry is illustrated in the following suggested factors: (1) the importance of subject-matter mastery (e.g., acquisition of verbal mediators and structure of knowledge), (2) heuristic procedures (e.g., use of analogy, "brainstorming," examination of limiting conditions) and (3) self-knowledge (e.g., psychoanalysis, revealing irrational personal elements which restrict pursuit of inquiry). The method of discovery, of course, can be considered as one part of the process of inquiry.

The Method of Discovery in the Teaching of Different Subject Areas

Teachers of mathematics have long used discovery methods in which they direct the learner's attention to selected data. The learner is expected to infer from these data and to make a response which, if correct, is confirmed by the teacher. If the learner's experience is incorrect, the teacher presents new data which will allow the learner to arrive at the correct knowledge. The teacher knows the discovery in advance of the learner's efforts. It is a new discovery only in the sense that it is new to the learner. For instance, a beginner is asked to find what number belongs in the box $\square + 6 = 15$ to make a story true. Such exercises are supposed to lead to discovery of the inverse relationship between addition and subtraction. Variation among discovery methods in mathematics center around the number of times the learner is to act upon the discovery before verbalizing the item of knowledge discovered: "When two groups are put together, if you know how many are in Group 1 and how many there are all together, you subtract to find out how many are in Group 2."

By way of contrast, in telling (non-discovery method), the teacher usually states the generalization first, illustrating it with examples, followed by the learner's applying the generalization to new problems.

Classroom learning by discovery in history and in social studies is similar although usually in these courses the method is subsumed under the words "problem-solving." The following illustration has been provided:

Let us, suppose a world history classroom in which students have encountered, during the reading of the assignment . . . the extreme of apparently useless information: "Alexander crossed the Hellespont with 35,000 men and began the series of conquests that quickly made him master of Darius' empire.". . . The teacher raises the question, "Could that sentence be a misprint? Surely, it doesn't sound reasonable that 35,000 troops could conquer a land containing many millions of people!"

That much is enough to get the flow of student hypotheses started. "Maybe there weren't so many people in those days." Investigations will bear this out, but not in sufficient degree to explain Alexander's conquests. "Maybe his army increased as he went along." Investigations support this also—at least, a student can readily find out that Alexander trained some 30,000 of his conquered subjects in Macedonian military techniques—but again the explanation is quantitatively inadequate. "Maybe the people had no weapons." But Macedonian weapons were not particularly complicated, as the student can easily discover. Vast numbers of people armed with only equipment for hunting, farm implements, clubs, and stones could make a fair showing against a small army. However, a new question could be introduced by the teacher, namely, "Why didn't Darius see to it that every household contained the simple weapons of his day?". . .

Sooner or later, someone will discover that the ordinary inhabitant of an Asiatic empire never took part in wars at all—that he apparently cared not at all who ruled over him. By the time a student has found out why, and has come to compare the passive hopelessness of the natives of Persia with the vigorous self-defense against Persia carried on by the Greek cities a century and a half earlier, and perhaps even to wonder what had enabled Alexander to conquer these same Greek cities, the comparison with the present scene will become painfully obvious. The state of affairs in India, in Burma, in Egypt, in Malaya, will have become relevant to the idea under discussion, which is no longer Alexander but rather the proposition, "People who believe that they have no stake in their government will not fight to maintain it. . . ."[1]

Discovery in art acquires a meaning different from the notion that there is a truth or criterion for truth (known to the teacher) which the learner himself can discover. Art as a human activity is concerned with creating something which has not existed before. The teacher cannot have prior knowledge of the learner's creation, and he might have trouble specifying in advance criteria for judging the creation, since criteria for judging creations vary. The imagination of the work, involvement of the student's own feelings and ideas in the product, and traditional standards such as "balanced contrast" are some criteria used. The difficulty of justifying whether or not a student has indeed created an artistic truth (e.g., a painting or a poem of value) is linked to the problem of a method which will enable one to create. Although the variables which might compose such a method have not been established, skill in handling media and techniques, conditions related to personality dimensions of conflict, reception, and factors of sensitivity to one's own action, as well as experiment have been suggested as relevant.

Many curriculum developments calling for the discovery method, as well as other procedures for conducting inquiry, are found in the teaching of science. Students who complete modern courses in science are supposed to demonstrate ability to apply this content (key concepts) of science to unfamiliar situations, to

---

[1] A. F. Griffin, "A Philosophical Approach to the Subject-Matter Preparation of Teachers of History." Unpublished doctoral dissertation, Ohio State University, 1942, 179–81.

suggest new lines of investigation, and to draw valid conclusions from observations and data. To these ends, students are to discover how the laws of science grow out of attempts to describe the observed phenomena of nature and to try their own hands at formulating tentative descriptions, examining them as new facts appear. Teachers of the new programs are admonished (a) to represent the spirit and method of science in classroom procedure, (b) to help the learner discover new ways of organizing knowledge, and (c) to aid self-directed learning on the part of the student. These admonitions are accompanied by the warning that the teacher will not be able to help students learn by the discovery method unless the teacher knows a number of different ways by which the principles to be discovered can be found (guided discovery). A central feature of newer courses in science is the introduction of laboratory work as a tool for the *generation* of ideas, not just for their verification. Problems and exercises are to lead the student into inference and interpretation as well as practice in reasoning with basic ideas. The purposes of the experiment are given, but students are encouraged to do as much as possible with a minimum of direction and to extend the inquiry on their own initiative. Likely difficulties are pointed out to the student and suggestions concerning extensions and variations of the experiment are made.

Advantages of Discovery Learning

1) Discovery learning overcomes the defect of vagueness. The learner's comprehension of a term is greater, because the learner has had first-hand experience with many objects, instances, parts, elements, and the like, which are combined to form the term or generalization. The primary fundamental ideas in any field, unless it be mathematics, are derived from objects. Therefore, familiarity with the objects gives significance to the idea. However, this is not to say that because all concepts are the results of human experience, they must be learned in much the same manner as mankind developed them.

2) It is sometimes said that those things one discovers for himself will be remembered better. The partial truth of this state-

ment might be explained by the amount of time spent on a task of discovery (overlearning) as opposed to a task which calls for less attention. Also, information acquired as a result of one's own search may be more closely related to the knowledge or impression already within a learner's repertoire. A new idea is not remembered so well if it is not linked to ideas already held. Perhaps the learner can do such linking better than a teacher who does not know what ideas the learner initially possesses.

3) The discovery method aids in transfer of learning by equipping one to deal with changed conditions. Practice in trying to use in new situations skills or ideas already mastered can lead to discovery and transfer of ideas. To the extent that the given knowledge or skills are unchanged by the learner as he greets different conditions in the new situation, there is likely to be failure. In this event, the learner must be taught that when failure occurs, he should analyze the conditions of the new task, explain the principal differences between it and previous tasks, and refashion his original knowledge or skill (discovery). In other words, although training for transfer may start with a telling method, it can offer opportunity for application of a discovery method: learner is (a) given knowledge of general principles, (b) asked to apply these principles to specific tasks, (c) makes errors or failures, (d) analyses the new task, and (e) formulates new generalizations.

4) The discovery method is consistent with valued autonomy of character and motivation. If one approaches learning tasks with the idea of discovering something rather than being told something, he is acting as an autonomous judger of success (intrinsically motivated) rather than dependent upon another's authority (extrinsically motivated). Thus, discovery learning is valuable as an end (autonomy) as well as a means (a way to learn).

Limitations of the Method

1) The inductive method requires much time, especially if guided discovery is not practiced. Observation and analysis are

slow processes. A deductive method or the making of generalizations at second-hand in their perfected form is much more expeditious when it can be shown that either method can result in the learner's attainment of the instructional objective. Parenthetically, some have speculated that success attributed to the discovery method is due to the increased time given to an aspect of subject matter rather than to the method itself.

2) The learner does not discover unless he is prepared to discover. The more one knows about the pattern of particular subject matter (even when deductively acquired), the more frequently will he recognize new instances and extensions of that subject matter. One needs to be equipped with criteria for knowing whether or not a truth has been discovered and to have a basis for deciding whether or not a problem has been solved.

3) Empirical evidence does not support the consistent efficacy of pupil discovery over direct and detailed instruction. Neither is there conclusive evidence that the discovery method is more effective for brighter pupils and the telling method more effective with less able ones. There is opinion that the learner's employment of the discovery method, especially if relatively unguided and with little chance of success, leads to the learning of errors, to frustration and withdrawal, and to other miseducative consequences.

Recommendations

The presence or absence of discovery learning is an insufficient criterion for the assessment of teaching and instructional materials. School officials should instead focus their attention upon changes they seek to effect in learners and collect evidence of the degree to which these changes occur and are retained. The discovery method, as well as other methods, should be used when directly related to the changes sought. The discovery method is probably unnecessary if the school system is only interested in knowing whether learners at the end of a period of instruction can (a) recall a conclusion or rule discovered by others, (b) describe the process which led to a recognized discovery, or (c) outline the major schemes (theories and generalizations) which are used in studying phenomena or solving problems.

Although the discovery method may aid in helping the learner apply in new situations the conclusions or generalizations of others, time spent in applying the rule or concept may be even more effective. Practice with the method of discovery is probably most necessary if it is expected that the learner will be able to formulate new rules or generalizations from particular instances. Keep in mind, however, that the ability to formulate new rules or solutions is the result of a great many factors (many of which are not yet identified) loosely termed the "process of inquiry" and that it will not be achieved by reliance on a single method of presentation.

Additional Readings

Ausubel, D. P., "Learning by Discovery," *Educational Leadership,* **XX,** Nov. 1962, 113–17.

Bruner, J. S., "The Act of Discovery," *Harvard Educational Review,* **XXXI,** I, Winter 1961, 21–32.

————, *The Process of Education.* Cambridge, Mass.: Harvard University Press, 1961.

Craig, R. C., *The Transfer Value of Guided Learning.* New York: Columbia University, Teachers College, Bureau of Publications, 1953.

Kersh, B. Y., and Wittrock, M. C., "Learning by Discovery: An Interpretation of Recent Research," *The Journal of Teacher Education,* **XIII,** 4, Dec. 1962, 461–68.

Ray, W. E., "Pupil Discovery versus Direct Instruction," *The Journal of Experimental Education,* **XXIX,** 3, March 1961, 271–80.

II. Programed Learning

THE WORDS "PROGRAMED LEARNING" bring to mind the following associations: teaching machines, a step at a time, each one going at his own pace, Socratic method, immediate knowledge of results, and active responding. If this chapter were written and arranged in the form of programed learning, the reader would behave in a predetermined manner after exposure to its content. The programer would assume responsibility for making explicit the behavioral changes to be wrought by the chapter and would collect evidence that the chapter brought about those changes in the population of readers for whom the chapter was prepared. It would be easy to promise and to deliver the result that at the conclusion of the chapter the reader will be able to list two distinctive characteristics of programed learning. It would be quite easy, but would require a longer chapter to ensure that the reader could illustrate four psychological principles for the construction of programed materials.

The reader may relax. This chapter is not programed. Your behavior is not being "shaped" in that there are no particular responses or quality of responses which you will be required to make after reading the chapter. Most conventional textbooks, films, teachers, and other instructional media seldom take responsibility for changing another's behavior. Most teaching-learning media merely present ideas, content, and make the assumption that the learner has the background necessary to find his own "meaning" and profit in the material. Almost never is an attempt made to collect evidence that instruction alone is successful in effecting predetermined change in the learner. Not so with pro-

13

gramed learning. The program is responsible for delivering promised changes. The essence of this new instructional procedure is twofold:

1) There is precision in stating the behavioral changes or outcomes that will occur following the use of the program. "The ability to indicate logical fallacies in arguments" is an example of the kind of specific outcome which a program could produce and for the development of which the programer could assume full responsibility. There is a misbelief that programed learning fosters only rote learning and memorizing of facts. Programed learning can and often does foster the ability to explore a discipline on one's own initiative and to discover basic principles. Analysis of prerequisites to attainment of the objectives and provision for leading the learner to these objectives is the task of programing.

2) There is experimentation with a representative sample of learners for whom the behavioral change is intended. Experimentation is conducted under conditions similar to those expected in situations where the program is to be used. In other words, the specification of objectives and experimental evidence that the behavioral changes indeed do occur in the learner are two constants in programed learning.

For bringing about this behavioral change, a number of procedures can be used. For some changes and with some learners, a teaching machine may be most useful. There are programs by which learners reach particular objectives through carefully graduated sequences, frequent questioning, and provision in the program for the learner always to make the right response. Other programs make sure that learners obtain the outcome sought by permitting the learner to make an error and infrequently rewarding him for his efforts. New program techniques are being developed through the testing of psychological principles in practical school settings. Sometimes learners find that they can achieve new understandings, complex thought processes, and problem-solving skills by being exposed to a program which merely stipulates in detail the behavioral changes demanded and then indicates the sources of information available to the learner in controlling his own sequence of instruction.

The results of research in programed instruction are suggesting how we can write more effective textbooks and workbooks and what we must do to conduct ourselves as teachers if we are to attain more success with learners. For example, many studies with programed instruction have confirmed an old belief that learners improve markedly when they receive immediate knowledge of results from their efforts, a practice which is frequently lacking in the conventional classroom.

Responses from principals indicate that by 1965 programed learning will be used in some fashion in approximately 71 per cent of American elementary and 65 per cent of secondary schools. School people anticipate the popularity of programing in the belief that it will fulfill the following expectations:

1) Individualize instruction by permitting each student to progress at his own rate of speed and allowing pupils to select that subject matter which is most appropriate for their own purposes and abilities.

2) Help the learner in understanding particular ideas, terms, or problems encountered in his studies. For example, if in reading a textbook one finds that he requires a knowledge of statistics to comprehend a section of the text and he lacks such knowledge, a programed supplement to the text would be available to help him acquire the necessary understanding.

3) Reach the hard-to-teach by appealing to those hyperactive and aggressive youngsters who reject instruction from teachers and to those pupils who attain greater achievement in isolation, free from the distraction of peers, and who learn from things rather than persons.

4) Diagnose the pupil's performance on specific learning tasks, revealing deficiencies that require attention.

5) Test the effectiveness of different ways of presenting material to those with exceptional attributes, e.g., the deaf, mute, creative, blind, crippled, psychotic, and culturally deprived.

6)   Teach the learner who is confined to home because of health. Also, one who has been absent may be able to "catch up" through programed lessons available upon his return.

7)   Give necessary background instructions to the "new arrival," the one who recently has moved into the school district and requires supplementary assistance.

8)   Aid in the re-education of teachers by helping them understand the changes in content and methodology of new curriculum.

Presently, there are insufficient programed materials to minimally satisfy these requirements of the schools. There is a deficiency in both number and quality of programs. It is true that already young children have learned to read through programed instruction (and without the assistance of a teacher). Others have achieved new competencies in spelling, foreign languages, science, and mathematics. Adolescents and adults have greatly benefitted from programs selected from the more than 350 currently offered. There are programs especially suited for the bright, average, and retarded student. There are programs designed for the secondary, primary, pre-school, adult, professional, and vocational levels. Incidentally, the junior high learner has commanded the most attention from the programer.

Programs represent a wide range of content; in mathematics they go from simple arithmetic through logic and computer programing; programs in English feature a variety of subject matter from traditional grammar to linguistics, punctuation to poetry. Through programing, many have acquired new understandings of such scientific topics as klystrons, dinosaurs, insects, bird migrations, weather, sound, rockets, latitude and longitude, photosynthesis, atomic theory, chemical bonding, and action of forces. Content from the behavioral and social sciences has been introduced to learners through programs like "Africa" and "physiological psychology." Most of these programs are units of instruction rather than semester or year-long courses. Only a small percentage of programs offer over 100 hours of instruction.

The evidence is clear that students indeed learn from programs; what is also important, they are learning by themselves.

Evidence from research studies has been most favorable to the effectiveness of programed learning in comparison to learning under conventional classroom instruction. This is not to say that all programs are effective. Some marketed products called "programs" by their advertisers are not programs at all. These artificial programs present a series of questions and answers which superficially appear to be programs in that they require constructed responses, a filling in of blanks, or provide immediate knowledge of results (a correct answer). Many of these so-called programs do not identify the new things a learner will be able to do and know at the conclusion of the program. Further, they only test; they do not teach. Often, they do not inductively lead the learner to note similarities and differences; do not help him attend to subtle cues which are important in formulating new concepts; do not help students to think abstractly, failing to develop meaning for terms which mediate between specific instances (explain their connection). Poor instructional materials do not demand that the learner make only responses which are relevant to the instructional task; they do not make order out of disorder. A quack program does not provide sufficient opportunities for the learner to practice the behavior desired. Most important, a poor program does not give the information and prerequisite behavior which will enable one to make desired responses and attain instructional objectives.

Many programs are downright boring. Authors have not broken out of a stereotyped pattern set by programing pioneers. The imaginative use of color, sound, humor, animation, and a host of other variables has appeared infrequently.

Too many programs have been produced in printed form rather than as film strip and sound. There has been a general failure among programers to recognize that one of the largest populations of learners is especially responsive to pictures and accompanying sound and that a sizable number of learners avoid printed material. The notion of presenting programed materials via television and film has not caught on even among those responsible for the production of mass media. This is unfortunate because experiments featuring audio-visual techniques have demonstrated the fruitfulness of combining audio-visual mechanics and programing.

Recommendations

1) School officials must be regenerative consumers. They must demand quality programs for a variety of tasks. Specifications given by school administrators should include the following:

a. Subject-matter areas which should be developed as complete courses, extending in time over one or more years. There is danger that the random survey of too wide a range of topics will lead to memorization of unrelated facts rather than to an understanding of basic principles involved.

b. Topics which should be treated as units of instruction and used for supplementary purposes in the classroom.

c. Statement of instructional objectives to be attained by learners through programed materials. A chief criticism of programing (e.g., "the programing scandal") is that too often programs offer content and behavior which is not appropriate in light of new knowledge and social conditions. It is miseducative to base the objectives of programed materials exclusively on the content found in existing textbooks rather than considering what subject-matter specialists deem to be most necessary for greeting that part of the environment with which their specialties deal. If school people do not want to reduce their schools to "fact dispensaries," they should specify that programs equip learners to look at evidence, consider relevancies, and recognize unstated assumptions. School leaders should make it known that they want programs which will change children into imaginative actors in particular areas of study. In communicating this desire, educators will need to have a picture of what children do when they show such behavior.

d. Economic requirements. The average cost per program is $10 to $15. Many of these programs can be put on film strip and sound tape or disc. An audio-visual format for group presentation could be especially economical. Surprisingly, for attaining most objectives there is little difference in the efficiency of learning under forced pacing, where one goes at a speed set by the programer, and individual pacing, where one goes at this freely chosen pace. In using programs which are film and sound, reusable, and can be shared with many, schools will find programed instruction less expensive than consumable workbooks or textbooks for each learner.

Budgetary considerations of programed learning should take into account the saving of instructional and learning time, the degree of mastery of learning, and the retention of learning which accompany the newer technique. The high cost of producing and testing programs makes their wide use desirable. Today, development of a one-year program costs $25,000 to $50,000. Programs of high quality can be available to schools at low cost when they are widely used.

e. Evaluative criteria. Professional organizations have made lists of questions to ask before buying programed materials. Most of these lists contain such questions as: (1) What is the intended student population? (2) What are the prerequisite courses? (3) What are the qualifications of your authors? (4) How and where was the program tested?

It is appropriate that school officials be familiar with and use these criteria, but it should be remembered that one will never find a perfect program. The goodness of a program depends upon the objectives held, the population of learners, and the conditions in which it will be offered. It looks as if programed materials will be subjected to higher standards of appraisal than any other instructional media. If textbooks, films, and teachers themselves had to pass the proposed standards, schools would be paragons of virtue or closed for lack of qualified instruction—most likely, the latter.

2) In-service education of teachers should feature the development and use of programed learning. The author of a nationally used program received two reports concerning its effectiveness. One school system was glowing in its praises. Children enjoyed the programed learning and mastered the objectives. The other system reported children's indifference and failure rate. Many explanations exist for this discrepancy, and most of them go back to the kind of introduction teachers gave the materials. If a teacher does not understand programing, fears and dislikes it, pupils under

that teacher's direction will probably fail to learn or will learn exceptionally well from the program, depending upon their desire to please or thwart the teacher. The acceptance or rejection of any instructional innovation depends upon the attitude and kind of influence generated by the instructional leader who introduces it.

Through development and tryout of a short programed lesson, teachers can learn the importance of stating objectives that are observable in pupil behavior and some of the multiple considerations required in bringing a learner to a desired state. Also, teachers can see ways in which programing enhances their role in making instructional decisions. In-service education in programing should prepare the teacher for new responsibilities in diagnosing learning difficulties, matching pupils to programs, and helping learners to apply the knowledge gained by the program to their own particular situations and purposes. Given programs which are consistent with the teacher's own instructional objectives and which help him with his own problems in the classroom, there is little opposition by teachers to the innovation.

3) Opportunities for experiments using programed learning should exist in schools. Too often school officials demand a new breakthrough in instructional practice without accepting any of the risks involved in its discovery. "What we need is a brand new idea that has been thoroughly tested." For the same reasons that medicine and engineering take big chances in allotting a percentage of their budgets to inquiry and experimentation, so should school systems permit a number of their classrooms to be laboratories for investigations of the mental process. To be on the move, a school system should invite qualified educational researchers (those who are concerned with the problems of instruction and possess intellectual tools for tackling these problems) into their classrooms for the purpose of testing hypotheses about the relations of presentational variables, subject matter, and the characteristics of particular learners. Perhaps the greatest contribution of programed learning is that it permits the systematic manipulation of instructional procedures and identification of the consequences which follow these procedures.

Additional Readings

Deterline, W. A., *An Introduction to Programed Instruction.* Englewood Cliffs, New Jersey: Prentice-Hall, Inc., 1962.

Fine, B., *Teaching Machines.* New York: Sterling Publishing Co., Inc., 1962.

Lysaught, J. P. and Williams, C. M., *A Guide to Programmed Instruction.* New York: John Wiley and Sons, Inc., 1963.

Mills, A. L. (editor), *Programmed Learning and the Educational Process.* Stanford, California: Thomas Alva Edison Foundation, Inc., 1961.

Phi Delta Kappan, special issue on programed instruction. Vol. XLIV, No. 6, March 1963.

Programs, '63, A Guide to Programed Instruction Materials Available to Educators by September 1963. Center for Programed Instruction, Inc., and U.S. Department of Health, Education, and Welfare, Office of Education, 1963.

Schramm, W., *The Research on Programmed Instruction—An Annotated Bibliography.* Stanford, California: Institute for Communication Research, Stanford University, 1962.

III. Knowledge and Learning

LEARNING IS BOTH a verb and a noun, a process and a product. We say one is learning or is undergoing instruction (process), and we say one has learned or possesses learning, has acquired knowledge (product).

School leaders have placed much emphasis upon the psychology of learning, upon ways for speeding up the time required for the acquisition of learning. They have been interested in new teaching techniques and new instructional materials which will help one learn more effectively. Only recently have they begun to consider an alternative approach to the problem of "so much to learn and so little time in which to learn." This alternative is philosophical rather than psychological, in that it seeks to resolve the problem by focusing upon the basis for classifying kinds of knowledge and the criteria by which statements are justified as knowledge as opposed to opinion. The psychological approach is more concerned with the dynamics of learning. Instead of laboring hard to equip learners with all knowledge (obviously impossible), or with any information which happens to be of importance to a pressure group or which has become entrenched as one of the traditional offerings of the school, officials are being asked to put the learners in possession of that knowledge which (a) can be applied in a wide range of situations, (b) is less likely to require unlearning, (c) will facilitate new learning, and (d) is unlikely to be available any place other than in school.

Persons making decisions in curriculum today are expected to seek economy in learning by selecting those general concepts, principles, and methods which allow one to handle more experience than that present in the immediate instructional environment. This is in contrast to the practice of heaping up piles of information which can be used only in limited situations like quiz programs or reporting the news of the day. What are the characteristics of these powerful general ideas? Where are they found? How do we select from the abundance of intellectual tools available?

Two Sources for "Powerful" Ideas

The universal ideas in our culture are sought in two places: (a) those branches of philosophy in which specialists give major attention to the nature of knowledge itself, and (b) the separate disciplines, such as mathematics, linguistics, and physics which develop their special "languages" (concepts, hypotheses, theories, methods) for dealing with a range of specifics in the aspect of life which is the province of the particular discipline. Linguists, for example, have universal general notions which are especially appropriate for describing, explaining, and predicting phenomena of language where it may occur. Techniques such as "contractive analysis," terms such as "phoneme" and "morpheme," and the new kit of intellectual tools which constitute modern syntax are economical because such techniques and symbols are widely applicable in problems involving language. Likewise, physicists find it possible to relate many specific instances of the physical world in fruitful ways because of general ideas (abstractions) like mass, energy, motion, and space, which have been constructed for interpreting man's physical environment. This is not to say that ability to describe and explain such aspects of the environment as language and physical events automatically ensures ability to apply this knowledge in complex problems of everyday life. Knowledge of the reasons for or explanations of right behavior does not necessarily lead to right actions. One can describe language correctly but not be able to communicate through language more effectively than another who has mastered the art (practice) but not a science (theory) of language.

Disciplines as a Game

One way to view a discipline is to regard it as a "game"—a game in which there is a purpose, objects to which the players attend, rules for playing the game, and ways for deciding whether a point has been made (a "truth" discovered). A discipline only exists when it has formulated its principles and rules of inquiry and when it produces new knowledge. This requires (a) agreement as to the classes of phenomena for which members of the discipline will take responsibility, (b) agreement on the concepts considered relevant, and (c) rules for stating when evidence (proof) has been shown.

There are many separate disciplines (games). One scholar lists nearly one thousand. Disciplines are born and die. They are born when there is need for the production and ordering of facts now not available. They die when they no longer simplify our understanding of an aspect of life (i.e., do not direct attention to important elements, do not give ways for relating these elements, and do not generate new questions for investigation).

A discipline is knowledge organized for efficient learning. The learner can see parts related to a whole because of the structure of the game. Further, the structure allows him to fit new parts into the whole when certain conditions are met, thereby giving these particulars greater meaning. In history, for example, one can effect linkage of events through interpretation made possible by such concepts as tragedy, the distribution of power, and universal activities of societies.

The Disciplines Approach Is not Traditional

Society has not yet become fully aware that the introduction of "disciplines" to the schools represents a dramatic change in education. On quick glance, many assume that the disciplines approach is but a return to subject matter, a much-needed correction from excessive emphasis upon the interests of the learner and passing aspects of contemporary life. On the other hand, some applaud its introduction because it suggests a way of preventing the subject-matter specialist from becoming narrow. They believe that when a specialist in the disciplines attempts to apply his special materials to schools, in which he must adapt content to human nature and the things of daily life, scholarship will become more convergent to the interests of the mass of men.

Something is missing in both of these views. The current disciplines approach represents more than a return to subject matter and application of the results of special research to educational ends. Its distinguishing characteristic is that it moves not the mere results of research, but investigations, methods, ideas, and principles of the disciplines, to the classroom itself. In a limited degree, research centers are to be extended from places like the university to include the common school. The child will be started on the most advanced plane, with the least to unlearn and correct as regards both particular things and method; with the maximum of attainable accuracy and with a selection of ideas and principles in some ratio to their importance and future fertility. The learning opportunities and activities offered to little children will remain quite concrete and manageable, but they will be related to sophisticated concepts.

The teaching and learning of a discipline, rather than the mastery of facts is at the center of the current revolution in curriculum. Newer courses of study in physics, biology, mathematics, history, anthropology, and other fields are intended to put students into the game as players, not as spectators. Learners are expected to act like physicists, biologists, mathematicians, historians, and anthropologists. The assumption is that by participating in the discipline the learners will subsequently follow developments in the fields with understanding and interest as citizens, and those few who continue their study of the game perhaps will add to knowledge as specialists in the years to come. In the new curriculum, learners are not just to talk about the conclusions (facts) produced in these disciplines, but possibly to engage in the production of such conclusions themselves and certainly to know the basis for calling the conclusion "fact." Economy of learning is believed to occur when one is taught how to acquire or justify facts rather than to recall facts. One way for teaching this is through discovery learning.

School men now have a choice: to introduce an unlimited

inventory of conclusions drawn from disciplines or to teach methods by which these conclusions are won and organized.

Selecting Disciplines for the Curriculum

> Good Heavens! Art is long,
> And short is our existence . . .
> How hard it is to win the means
> By which one rises to the sources!
> And 'ere he only gets half way
> Must a poor devil likely pass away![1]

It is impossible for an individual to delve very deeply into many disciplines. How shall those administering the curriculum decide upon the disciplines to offer? In answering this question three measuring rods for a curriculum are proposed: (a) comprehensiveness with respect to ways of arriving at or justifying truth or knowledge; (b) social utility, or the degree of usefulness of the discipline to all citizens; (c) prerequisite knowledge, selection on the ground that the standards and thought processes of certain disciplines are fundamental to others.

COMPREHENSIVENESS

If one assumes that the school exists to lead pupils to truth, to knowledge (knowledge defined as "justified belief" as opposed to mere opinion or guesses), then those disciplines which represent a range of ways for arriving at truth and justifying belief should be selected, rather than restricting selection to a nonrepresentative or unbalanced sample in which narrow criteria in justifying knowledge are used. Schools have been criticized for emphasizing scientific means for validating knowledge to the exclusion of other means. It is sometimes said that those leaving school hold that a statement is not true unless it has been verified by objective observation in which an expected occurrence conforms to measured actuality (a belief that only the method of science leads to truth). The acceptance of a single scientific criterion as the only criterion for defining truth is a restricted outlook and eliminates many cultural values.

[1] Johann W. Von Goethe, *Faust*, Part I, Scene 1, 1808.

In addition to preparing the learner to gain knowledge through the organs of sense and measurement, it is important that he be familiar with validation of truth through reason or logic. The foundations of mathematical systems and their validity, for instance, are dependent upon the latter road to truth. It can be argued that less accepted ways for establishing truth should also be in the repertoire of the learner. It may be desirable for him to recognize that knowledge is validated by some in terms of their own intuition (an immediate and direct knowledge of what one must do), through revelation (communication from the divine), and by recognition of their own existence (what I am and do is truth).

In any event, the pupil should learn that even those disciplines which do not permit all procedures to be used for justifying truth find the same procedures useful for discovering truth. The scientist uses reason as well as his senses and he is not indifferent to intuition; faith and reason have long been linked, and the religious belief that man does not possess ultimate truth is compatible with the scientist's striking out against a premature certitude.

In the interests of comprehensiveness, it would be appropriate for the school to sample disciplines which offer a range in emphasis they give to particular avenues for justifying knowledge. Art, with its concern for subjective validation, could balance a discipline in science. History could be taught to illustrate the criterion of (a) coherence (ideas have to fit together) and (b) verifiability (ideas have to be checked out in terms of past events). Also, philosophy could be introduced to show that in some fields it is important that a claimed truth does not conflict with previously established knowledge within the discipline or with justified beliefs in other fields. To learn that in religious experience appeal to authority is acceptable and that in the physical sciences an appeal to a sensory test is appropriate opens doors to the multiple aspects of living and permits one to integrate apparent contradictions.

SOCIAL UTILITY

Few would contend that it is enough for any discipline to be an end in itself. Specialists in each field have faith that many, if not all, of the discipline's truths have, or at some time in the future will have, relevancy to the problems of mankind. The phrase "knowl-edge for knowledge's sake" is not taken seriously.

This does not mean that all disciplines will serve equally well the educational needs of men in a given social context. Some specialties of very narrow scope have little to contribute to the problems which directly touch all lives. Conventionally, school subjects have drawn from the disciplines of English (literature, grammar, and composition); social science (history, government, economics, geography); mathematics; and natural science (biology, chemistry, physics). These fields are seen as carrying a content which develops a common past and common future outlook. Conclusions from these fields are regarded as indispensable in the proper discharge of one's functions as a citizen. Sometimes the arts (music, painting, drawing, modeling) are included in general education, but often the arts have been suspect because they tend to stress individuality rather than conformity to predetermined behaviors of organized society.

It should be noted, however, that school subjects have been composed of subject matter from disciplines but that the disciplines themselves (the habits of thought, the literature of the discipline, authorities in the field, and modes of inquiry) often were not taught. Learners were not expected to apply in their daily lives the methods of historians or physical scientists. Newer concepts of social utility (i.e., how to live with change) are redefining the school as an institution for training learners in the methods of correcting and extending knowledge rather than as a museum for the conservation of old truths. As this happens, newer disciplines which are resting their reputation on fruitfulness in inquiry may replace those which are valued more for the answers they transmit than the questions they raise. Psychology, for instance, is challenging literature for the honor of interpreting human nature. Parenthetically, it should be mentioned that English as a discipline has "fallen apart." A response to social demands for application of language, composition, and literature has resulted in the fragmentation of knowledge in the field. At present, it is doubtful that specialists in English can affirm that "English" meets an essential criterion for a discipline: *an internal organiza-tion of subject matter suitable for efficient learning.*

It is difficult to defend the choice of a discipline on the grounds that it is higher in the hierarchy of fields relevant to problems in the social order. Each social science, for example, has a unique function in its power to direct investigations of importance to society. It will be difficult for many school leaders to separate their evaluation of school subjects as traditionally taught from the disciplines themselves. "History" as a traditional school sub-ject and "history" as a field of knowledge may carry the same label, but there is a world of difference in their value. Therefore, when one is asked to consider disciplines like history or geogra-phy, he should not assume that this means the transmission of content which will indoctrinate learners with facts biased by a particular nation. For instance, warlike nations have long stressed history and geography, but there is nothing inherent in these two fields which precludes there being used for the purpose of culti-vating more socialized intelligence. As disciplines, history and geography can help learners to apply canons of evidence, distrust simple solutions, and recognize the connection between fact and value. As traditional school subjects, history and geography in-doctrinate learners in accordance with a preferred social attitude. Learners come to believe that the facts and events of history are consistent in supporting the particular bias or value prevailing in the community where the instruction is being offered. As a result of the stacking of facts by teacher or text to support a proposition or premise about what *should* go on in society, the pupil finds it difficult to distinguish fact from value. Furthermore, he is unable to reconcile the facts he has learned to parrot with newer histori-cal and geographical knowledge as it is produced by the scholar.

On the other hand, anthropology and sociology have seldom appeared in the traditional school program. The present demand that citizens have a world view will result in the introduction of these fields into the curriculum. History can do the job, but to many pupils it is only seen as reflecting parochial interests. It may be easier to effect the development of objectives demanded for an expanding world through disciplines like anthropology which already are popularly characterized as having broad conceptions about world culture and social institutions.

Sociology, like history, has been stereotyped. By pronounced attention to the phenomenon of social disorganization sociologists have given the impression that sociology is more devoted to the improvement of social institutions than to preservation of those institutions as they are.

PREREQUISITE KNOWLEDGE

Prerequisite knowledge is related to the curricular problem of sequence, the ordering of content for effective learning. Among principles of such ordering are those which say the learner should proceed from (a) the simple to the complex, (b) the familiar to the unfamiliar, and (c) the past to the present. Those who hold the view of a logical dependency of knowledge, as opposed to the ordering of knowledge on the basis of assumed interest of learners or practices in social problems, reject the traditional pattern of teaching biology as the first course in the secondary school curriculum in science. They maintain that understanding of biology is dependent upon prior understanding of the principles of chemistry and that understanding of chemistry best occurs after one has acquired the basic concepts of physics. One older view was that biology was of more general interest and value to learners than physics or chemistry and, therefore, should be taught earlier. Even the person who would drop out after the tenth grade could profit from biology. The modern view, more concerned with the mastery of science, holds that the ordering of topics or subjects must follow the development of essential principles and terms, not the presumed interests of pupils. However, to the extent that physics, unlike biology, requires prior mastery of mathematical tools, the traditional practice of teaching biology first, while mathematical skills were being developed, had some logical validity.

The determination of prerequisites on the basis of dependency occurs through an analysis of an ultimate objective (a task analysis) in which one asks "What understanding and skills must one bring with him if he is to successfully participate in the learning opportunities intended?"

At an elementary level, it is commonly said that the ability to read, write, and compute to a minimum competency is basic to successful participation in formal educational activity. These skills are first in order because of their wide application to more specialized divisions of knowledge. However, "wide applicability" and the disciplines must be looked at in at least three ways. Some disciplines serve other disciplines by becoming an element within these diverse fields. Mathematics, for instance, is an important tool within science as well as a discipline in its own right. Other disciplines have wide applicability in that they show the relations of diverse fields to each other, thereby illuminating the significance of the respective fields. Philosophy as a synthesizing discipline combines the relevant parts of various fields of knowledge; religion as a comprehensive life orientation coordinates the efforts of all fields by raising the ultimate questions of existence, e.g., physical science and the intelligibility of the universe, social science and the nature of freedom, literature and the meaning of death and tragedy.

Scholars in a field like history absorb many disciplines in their effort to interpret events. In so doing, workers in this field demonstrate the wide applicability of history as an integrating discipline.

Lacking experimental evidence in support of any principle for the ordering of disciplines, the curriculum leader might well recommend the early introduction of two disciplines, philosophy and mathematics. Philosophy would orient learners to the fields of inquiry. More efficient learning might occur if learners were prepared to see similarities and differences among the factual disciplines which they will meet later. Just as familiarity with maps of the world may enhance one's perspective of a particular part of the world, so a description of the essential features of several disciplines may help to make order out of chaos brought by increasing specialization. To the extent that philosophy leads to an understanding of the general features of any and all sciences, it could be a fundamental foundation for learning.

In the second discipline proposed for inclusion, mathematics, an abstract structure and pattern finds wide use. Much time is required to bring the learner to knowledge of what numbers are and to develop the ability to apply symbolic forms and transformations in new situations. Therefore, it might be especially desirable to begin this most abstract and general discipline at an early age.

Differences Between Concepts *in* a Discipline and Concepts *About* a Discipline

Earlier it was mentioned that powerful concepts for pursuing inquiry were found in the separate disciplines and that general concepts about the disciplines were found in that branch of philosophy which is concerned with the nature of knowledge itself. Concepts about a discipline are of a different order from concepts necessary for pursuing inquiry in a field. The former are sometimes termed "the language of the onlooker," whereas the latter are termed "the language of the participant."

A contrast between the two languages can be seen in these illustrations with respect to sociology. Terms such as "role," "status," "social class," "sanction," "function," and "authority" have technical meanings which are useful for one who would look at the environment as a sociologist. These "verbal mediators" direct attention to elements within a society and the social forces which would not be apparent without these "constructs." The usefulness of these concepts is shown when they enable the participant to describe and explain group behavior wherever it occurs (i.e., in family life, in government, in schools, in modern cities, or in remote areas). On the other hand, there are concepts *about* sociology. For example, there is the notion that sociology is concerned with inquiry into how activities of men maintain or change the social system in which they live, and there is the generalization that sociologists are concerned with the regularities of observable behavior of human groups. To say that sociologists acquire their knowledge through the methods of science (through systematic theory and empirical validation) is another way for talking *about* this discipline. Knowledge about the "game" of sociology does not qualify one to be a player in sociology any more than knowledge about baseball signifies that one is in the game rather than being a spectator.

This is not to say that knowledge *about* a field is of less value than knowledge *in* a field. There is no hierarchy of values between these two kinds of knowledge. Both have unique functions to perform. Concepts about knowledge are valuable in helping one comprehend the field in which he proposes to labor. How sad it is to see one who has studied for years in a field and has so lost himself in a mass of activities and details that he is unable to bring its cognitive elements into a common framework and to use its principles in starting new inquiry within the domain of the discipline.

One who would be a wise consumer of a discipline rather than a producer will find that knowledge about knowledge has special value. This is true for learners in school as well as for curriculum planners. A broad-scale map of knowledge, as opposed to a detailed one, is designed for the purpose of understanding the way human knowledge is organized, what to expect from particular specialists, and the range of knowledge available.

Indication of such understanding would be the ability to identify and respond appropriately to the common features by which items are grouped as belonging to a field. It is important to learn that no material is chemical, artistic, or psychological in itself, but becomes chemical, artistic, or psychological when it stimulates particular kinds of questions and responses. After learning how to identify instances, say, of the class "art objects," the successful learner can find new examples of this class and greet them with expectancy developed for the class. Economy of learning has occurred when one responds in a correct fashion to a new instance of the class.

Recommendations

1) The academic disciplines and knowledge about knowledge should be introduced as complements to the traditional content of school subjects. This does not mean that one can "cover" all traditional content and still develop competency in a discipline. Much content must be acquired by the learner on his own after he learns how to learn the subject matter, rather than taking school time for the dissemination of information which does not require systematic instruction. There are at least three serious criticisms of traditional schooling grounded in the acquisition of facts.

First, so great is the body of existing facts that learning composed of facts can only be unsatisfactorily selective.

Second, most masses of facts will soon be changed by new conditions and discoveries.

Third, recall and applications of learned facts alone will not lead to thought processes of judgment, inference, and reasoning which are demanded in problems of consequence to the individual and to groups.

Desire for the "power to deal with the techniques of tomorrow and not of yesterday" is changing our instructional materials and programs. Among the most significant of these changes is the introduction of the disciplines and the demand for knowledge about knowledge which enables the learner to understand the nature, problems, and application of major fields.

By way of example, pupils who have studied geography should be able to demonstrate that they can do the things that geographers do. School leaders should collect evidence that the pupil is able to prepare accurate maps from first-hand field observation; describe an area in which he has worked, making use of the standard conventions—criteria of selection and vocabulary of geographers; formulate geographic hypotheses and test these hypotheses in the light of data he is able to obtain. A far cry from the naming of capitals!

Recommendation that both academic disciplines and knowledge about knowledge become part of the curriculum is not to imply that all traditional content of the school need be eliminated. The disciplinary approach will be an additional part of the curriculum, but will not constitute the total curriculum.

Society will continue to demand that certain values or premises be presented as ends, to be accepted with little question. The premises of the Bill of Rights, for example, are seen as necessary ground rules for a pluralistic society and the school is regarded as an institution for systematic instruction in these rules. Likewise, strong arguments remain for transmitting particular exemplars in literature and history so that all citizens have at least some common cultural referents and shared experiences.

Neither need reorganization in behalf of the disciplines exclude the functional curriculum. Learners should be given opportunity to wrestle with vital intellectual issues and problems extending beyond the province of the disciplines. The organized-knowledge approach can be complemented by the study of complex problem areas like conservation of natural resources, community planning, and fundamental issues such as what the balance between government and individual responsibility should be. It is not enough (as has been the practice) for schools to pose problems that are crucial to all citizens and to expect pupils to be able to derive from academic scholars information that may contribute to the explanation or solution of these problems. In attacking a practical problem, one cannot get help from an academic discipline unless he knows what expertise lies in that discipline and can comprehend the information available. As schools teach a discipline, there can be a corresponding improvement in practical problem-solving. It should not be overlooked, however, that the disciplinary approach means that explanations and conclusions are not to be transmitted independently of the way they were produced. The method of inquiry by which these conclusions were produced must itself be taught in order that the conclusion may be rightfully interpreted. Perhaps in this revolutionary approach, pupils will not only learn how to produce and validate new conclusions in the field of knowledge, but will discover a way to validate answers to problems in their daily lives.

Biologists, for instance, have contributed prospectuses of research for pupils in schools in order to give them experience in the art of investigation. These problems for investigation allow the possibility of the pupil's discovering a new fact, a new relationship, a new technique—something which no one has known before. Some idea of the range and kinds of problems undertaken by pupils can be seen in the following:

A. Animal Behavior

Reproductive Behavior of North American Sticklebacks—William L. Hartman

An introduction to observational and experimental research may be gained by an aquarium study of the reproductive behavior of North American sticklebacks. By observation are the reproductive behaviors of North American species the same as for *Gasterosteus aculeatus,* which also occurs in Europe? By experimentations do the same sign stimuli release similar behavioral responses in all species? A research approach is suggested and pertinent literature cited.

B. Ecology

Analysis of Bird Territory—Thomas G. Overmire

Ownership of an adequate territory seems to be a prerequisite for successful nesting for most species of birds. Yet the factors that determine what makes up an adequate territory are not well understood. Careful analysis of breeding populations should make it possible to define what the factors are.

C. Genetics

Detection of the Effects of Genes Carried in Heterozygous Condition—Richard C. Lewontin

Most known mutations in well-studied organisms are recessive to the wild type; they must be present in double dose (homozygous) for their effect to be observed. An organism that carries a recessive mutation in single dose, combined with a single dose of the wild type (heterozygous), appears normal. However, there are many examples where the presence of a recessive mutation in a single dose with the wild-type gene does alter the outward appearance of the organism. The effects of these genes in single dose are so subtle that they cannot be easily observed or detected. If we could develop a method of detecting the heterozygotes, it would be possible to use this technique in selection of agricultural breeding stock.[2]

New organizational structure should accompany the new content. Miel has called attention to the need for experimenters to ascertain the disciplines most suitable for different age levels, and the length of time required for pupils to attain a sufficient grasp of their content. She suggests that they be grouped in "families" and studied in a comparative manner as follows:

Proposed Cycles for Comparative Study of Disciplines

Cycle One

Grade 4—The arts (graphic and plastic, fine and industrial, music, dance, poetry)

[2] American Institute of Biological Sciences, Biological Sciences Curriculum Study, *Research Problems in Biology: Investigations for Students, Series 1.* New York: Doubleday & Company, Inc., Anchor Books, 1963.

Grade 5—The natural and physical sciences (human biology, physiology, chemistry, physics, physical geography, geology, climatology, astronomy) and mathematics (arithmetic, geometry, and algebra)

Grade 6—Social sciences (history, anthropology, sociology, economics, political science) and ethics

Cycle Two

Grade 7—Communication (linguistics, semantics, mathematics, statistics, art forms)

Grade 8—Social sciences (history, human geography, political science, economics)

Grade 9—Natural and physical sciences (biology, chemistry, and physics)

Cycle Three

Grade 10—Communication and aesthetics (literature and the arts)

Grade 11—Social sciences (sociology, psychology, social psychology, anthropology)

Grade 12—Religion, philosophy, and ecology[3]

The disciplines offered by Miel for selection sample all the chief branches of knowledge. Traditional subject-matter designation, such as "algebra" or "American literature," are replaced by courses generalized in nature, such as mathematics and literature. These disciplines illustrate the principle ways for investigating and validating truth; they also have social utility. The sample includes those fields which can serve excellently as foundations for deeper specialization. They also include religion and philosophy which integrate knowledge. The attainment of knowledge about knowledge, a broad and comprehensive perspective, extending into all major areas of the nature and process of the universe, might be realized by such a program.

Additional Readings

Broderick, Mary, "Toward a Fabric of Knowledge: Common Elements Among Fields of Learning," *The Educational Record*, Vol. 43, No. 3, 217–22.

[3] Alice Miel, "Knowledge and the Curriculum," ASCD Yearbook, 1963, Chapter 4.

Broudy, Harry S., B. Othanel Smith, and J. R. Burnett, *Democracy and Excellence in American Secondary Education.* Chicago: Rand McNally and Company, 1964.

Miel, Alice, "Knowledge and the Curriculum," Chapter 4, ASCD Yearbook, 1963, pp. 1–52.

The Nature of Knowledge: Implications for the Education of Teachers. Milwaukee, Wisconsin: The Edward A. Uhrig Foundation, 1961, 96 pages.

Phenix, Philip, "Key Concepts in the Crisis in Learning," *Teachers College Record,* December 1956.

———, *Philosophy of Education.* New York: Holt, Rinehart, and Winston, 1958.

———, "The Topography of Higher Liberal Learning," *Phi Delta Kappan,* Vol. XLI, No. 7, April 1960, pp. 307–12.

The Scholars Look at the Schools, A Report of the Disciplines Seminar, June 1961, National Education Association, 1962.

Ward, Virgil S., "The Role of Knowledge," in *Educating the Gifted— An Axiomatic Approach.* Columbus, Ohio: Charles E. Merrill Books, Inc., 1961, pp. 141–55.

PART II. SELECTING INSTRUCTIONAL OBJECTIVES

THE SELECTION of instructional objectives is both a matter of deciding about the ways we want our fellow man to act and choosing from among the vast cultural resources (thoughts, works, achievements) that must be transmitted to oncoming generations. This is not to say that cultural content is separate from action. Actions, too, can be part of the cultural heritage, just as knowledge (justification for beliefs) and the intellectual tools of civilization are indispensable for certain actions.

The following chapter indicates the importance of selecting objectives only after consideration of the particular learners, the social conditions in which our citizens are living and are likely to be living in the future, and the status of knowledge. Fruitful questions are posed which increase the choices available and lead to consistency and thoroughness as we decide which way our schools shall go.

IV. What Should Be Taught?

NO BOARD OF EDUCATION member, principal, or teacher can proceed far with intelligent plans for schooling until what is to be taught has been agreed upon. Teachers, textbooks, buildings, equipment, organization, and methods are appropriate only in the light of the objectives of instruction. Unfortunately, some prize artifacts of instruction without justifying these artifacts in terms of instructional purpose. A particular book, for example, may be purchased for the school because an influential person likes that book. Further, there is much conflict regarding the instructional purposes themselves. Conflict in the selection of objectives is usually cast around the giving of greater emphasis to our heritage of knowledge and information versus stress upon our heritage of action.

On the one hand, the school is asked to concentrate upon developing boys and girls who can recall and reflect upon various items of information and knowledge (knowing what). On the other hand, the school is expected to give major attention to developing those actions which characterize "the worthy person" (knowing how). The latter includes patterns of action in interpersonal relations that represent selected sentiments and values drawn from the culture's heritage of behavior. An objective that calls for the learner to work well with others while maintaining his own integrity is an example of an objective in the "knowing-how" domain. It might be illustrated by practices such as these: "able to act as a host or hostess for a group gathering," "will stand up against group leaders if he thinks they are wrong."

41

The following remarks by school board members are typical expressions of demands for knowing what as well as knowing how:

"I am concerned that our children do not show honesty and that our schools may be contributing to this state of affairs. Only this week I heard of another case of mass cheating in the classroom. The teacher left the room, and many pupils began to get answers from their friends. No wonder there is delinquency and loss of moral character in the land."

"Perhaps we shouldn't make it a policy that teachers proctor all examinations. Instead we might seek to develop honor among the pupils to prepare them so that they independently resist the temptation to cheat and that they do the right thing not because someone is watching, but because they know what is right and because they find satisfaction in doing just that."

"My concern is that our schools are not adequately teaching students how to write. Do you have any idea of the number of our graduates who fail college composition tests?"

"Before we get on results of examinations, I'd like to know what progress we're making in strengthening our program in history. If we taught more about our great historical forebears, there might be less need to worry about the character of today's youth."

"Not only the strengthening of history, but what is the status of getting new offerings into the curriculum? What additions have we made to the program in foreign language? What are we doing about teaching science in the elementary school?"

These board members are confusing means of instruction with ends of instruction. They should specify the behavior they seek in learners and apply evidence as to what experiences will produce this behavior. It would be important, for instance, to know whether a board member regards the acquisition of information about historical figures as a justified end in itself, or whether he is chiefly concerned about the conduct of learners in daily life and regards history as relevant to that end. If concerned about conduct, experiment might show that selected experiences in social relations as a substitute for the study of history will be more effective in producing the change desired. Often board members try to justify the introduction of traditional and personally valued content on the grounds that the mastery of this content is necessary to a more important goal. When they do so, their assumptions should be challenged. If not verified, the assumptions should be rejected or admitted as ends in themselves.

Analysis of the above conversations reveals other difficulties board members are having and suggests ways to redirect the discussion of what to teach.

Objectives versus Illusory Ideals

Aims like "character," "the worthy person," "good citizen," "self-realization" are not the equivalent of measurable objectives such as "the ability to recognize form and pattern in literary works as a means of understanding their meaning" and "the ability to make original interpretations of data drawn from particular subject matter." Evidence that the latter objective has been attained could, for instance, be collected from responses made by pupils in following these directions: "Write five statements that you are sure are true according to the facts given in these data." Aims or ideals such as "the worthy person" and "good character" serve the useful purpose of reminding educators that a difference exists between *what is* and what *might be,* that mankind, including schools and other institutions, has not arrived at perfection. These ideals are illusory in the sense that there is no agreement about how they can best be fulfilled and what would constitute evidence that they were indeed fulfilled. Fortunately, there are always those persons who have visions of how ideals might better be represented in daily life, thereby keeping present practices from becoming idols.

There is temptation for school teachers to seek public approval by indicating that they are developing the moral equivalent of "good citizenship" and "worthy persons." Examination of the actual test items used to measure that which is being taught by the claimants reveals that pupils are learning how to respond to numerous problems and situations of which the following are a sample:

"How would you prove experimentally that roots and stems act differently to the force of gravity?"

"George weighs 150% as much as Tom. George's weight is how many times as much as Tom's weight?"

"Which of these best indicates your character? Hands in work on time, doesn't waste school supplies, listens when someone is talking, and abides by group decision?"

There is no one-to-one correspondence between the specific abilities to use information demanded by such items and the abstract ideals for mankind. In stating that they are developing persons consistent with these ideals, school leaders give only a partial truth. The accumulation of many classroom "learnings" may be steps in the general direction of these ideals, but they never encompass all possible meanings of the ideals. Consequently, there is much antagonism against schools when pupils do not respond or act appropriately to all situations which permit expressing various interpretations of ideals.

The schools cannot have it both ways. Schools cannot claim credit for developing "citizenship," when they are obviously doing much less, without being charged with failure to develop citizenship when learners do not meet all expectations of citizenship current in the society.

The School Does Not Control Necessary Variables for Developing the Whole Child

We have said that schools err in stating they fulfill general ideals and in not making explicit the objectives for which they assume responsibility. Likewise, schools are at fault in accepting responsibility when they have little chance of meeting the responsibility. In the case of character education, for instance, there are at least three aspects to be considered: (a) intellectual—knowing what is right, (b) motivational—wanting to do what is right; and (c) behavioral—what is actually done. To effect achievement in each of these aspects is beyond the capacity of the school as now constituted. The home is by far the most powerful character-education agency. By the age of ten, whatever character the child has he is likely to have for life, and that kind of character represents the values of the home. The child is the direct product of the way his parents treat him. "As they are to him, so he is to all others." The basic trends in behavior acquired in the home may be strengthened by the school but not changed radically. If the schools were to be fully, rather than partially, responsible for the development of character in all youngsters, they would have to control the children from birth, acquiring full management of the environment of these children, manipulating parents or substituting for the parents.

This is not to say that the schools cannot equip pupils to verbalize "right behavior," to note inconsistencies between stated ethics and actual performance, and to make particular desired responses to a limited range of social situations. Pupils can learn not to look at one another's papers during examinations, but there is little likelihood that this learning will transfer to other situations demanding manifestations of honesty.

School leaders must recognize the differences between what the school *should* teach and what it *can* teach. Ideally, there are many ways in which learners should be changed. The absence of control of relevant variables such as time and persons significant to the learners limits achievement. This point can be made in reference to ultimate or future behavior on the part of the learner. Schools try to establish a logical relationship between what is taught in school and the kind of life the learner will lead as an adult. There is, however, little evidence the curriculum of the school determines one's conduct in all aspects of life as an adult. So many other educational agencies—television, church, newspaper, and loved ones, for example—influence one's future that it is not possible to assume that the school in its limited way can fulfill a responsibility for determining the future life of the graduate.

Teaching versus Presenting

Many difficulties in discussion of the curriculum stem from failure to distinguish between teaching and presenting. Teaching is the deliberate attempt to change the learner's behavior in desirable directions. The behavior may be the ability either to state and apply knowledge or to demonstrate a certain pattern of action in daily life. The change sought is specified in advance and the teacher accepts responsibility for effecting this change. The teacher says "at the end of instruction, the learner must know these things (know that) and be able to do these things (know how)—knowledge that he does not now possess."

Sometimes the teacher says "I will not limit my responsibility by requiring that the learner make a particular response to a range of situations or problems, but will also see that he gives new responses to these problems—responses which I have not specified or taught but which meet the criteria for appropriate responses to such situations." Thus, teaching need not produce mere paired-associate or stimulus–response learning but can include the development of understanding and ability to discover new solutions to problems.

Presenting is the sharing or offering of particular values without accepting responsibility for the kinds of responses the learners make to these values. In presenting, there is no *explicit* intention of changing another's outlook, pattern of response, or general behavior. When pupils are confronted with beautiful paintings or literary exemplars, are taken on field trips to places like the seashore, or are addressed by famous personalities without the teacher's making an effort to develop the learners' responses to these cultural opportunities, there is no teaching—only the possibility of influence. As an example of presenting, a class may visit a jail, and each pupil may come away with different "learnings." One child may generalize that crime does not pay, another that society has not advanced far in its notions of personal rehabilitation, and another that he can beat the game as a criminal.

Under teaching, as opposed to presenting, all the members of the class would make the same generalizations or quality of generalization from the visit to the jail. If the teacher wanted pupils to give reasons as to why jails should be institutions for rehabilitation rather than institutions of punishment, the teacher would make sure arguments were received and reproduced by learners and that pupils were not left to formulate miseducative notions from the situation.

Teaching means accepting responsibility for changing another's behavior. Mere presentation is an easier task. When *not* teaching, one need only present stimuli which have been found to be of value to many distinguished persons and which are of presumed interest to the learner. But the burden of learning, e.g., how he responds to the situation or stimuli, is left to the pupil.

In conversations regarding curriculum, arguments arise because participants do not make clear whether the learning opportunity is to serve in teaching or whether it is to exist as a possible source for influence. Introducing pupils to historical accounts of events in the lives of great men is a case in point. Some will object to the presentation of these accounts without first knowing whether they are to serve as instrumentalities in teaching, in the deliberate shaping of learner behavior, e.g., ability of learner to describe historical purposes; or whether they are to be supplied as mere information from which any impression can be derived. Many things that are of value to mature citizens are of no value to those unprepared to receive them and to derive the appropriate generalization and affection from them.

Content Can Be Viewed as an Instrumentality for Attainment of Objectives or as an End in Itself

A chief source for disagreement in what to teach lies in the fact that many fail to see that a particular practice, artifact, bit of information, or course offering can be evaluated in terms of whether or not it contributes to a larger and more important purpose. Some have not learned to look for encompassing objectives of instruction but focus on the means of instruction as ends in themselves. The question, for instance, as to whether pupils should read *The Tale of Two Cities* or *War and Peace* should be decided not on the grounds that either of these books is a priority in its own right, but on whether one of these books will better help an individual pupil reflect on what it means to be a human being and raise crucial questions about the meaning of war, death, and friendship. So, too, with history—it is not so important that pupils can recall particular events about the period of Reconstruction or the Great Depression as that they be able to identify whether such events are interpreted in terms of social and national influences, personalities of men, or the hand of God. Historical events will be necessary to development of recognition of schemes for historical interpretation, and the events can be selected on the basis of interest to a particular people. However, the event introduced into the classroom will always be an inadequate historical sample. It is far more economical and intellectually honest to equip the learner to read and judge history independently

School men arguing over whether to offer physics, biology, chemistry, or general science to all learners might better regard these offerings as learning opportunities (means) and not objectives (ends). Their decisions should be made on the grounds that one of these subjects will be more effective in helping learners acquire scientific modes of inquiry.

Teachers have been criticized for treating classroom activities as ends. Children in the primary grades sometimes develop a model harbor, for instance, in which they construct various kinds of boats and facilities. In these settings, children learn about harbor rules and general shipping operations. One over-all purpose of the harbor unit is to further the concept of economic and social interdependency and the harbor is selected because of some presumed interest on the part of learners and the community. A harbor may be appropriate on the coast, whereas an agricultural unit would be better in a farming region. However, at times the construction activity becomes an end in itself. Harbor units are used in classrooms in which children have no interest in shipping and its facilities, and teachers do not sample the children's ability to identify the concept of interdependency in new situations following the activity.

The curriculum of the school may be uneducative when leaders assume that particular subject matter has virtues but make no effort to demonstrate these virtues. An extreme illustration would be teaching mathematics as a formal system and expecting the learner to behave more reasonably in his human relations. Likewise, there have been those who defended the offering of Latin on the grounds that it contributed to facility in English. Unless elements in Latin are directly related to behavior in English, there is little chance of establishing a causal connection between the two.

When an offering can no longer compete with others in the curriculum as an end, those with vested interests in this offering attempt to justify it as being relevant to demands in education. Seldom, however, do the defenders provide experimental evidence that the traditional content will contribute to attainment of priorities as well as the newer content will.

Recommendations

We contend that the curriculum of American schools will encompass at least three different kinds of instructional objectives. Each of these kinds of objectives is distinctive enough to warrant particular organizational patterns, instructional materials, and instruments of appraisal.

The categories of objectives are derived from several principal sources. One source is the learner himself. Not all learners require the same objectives. Objectives can be drawn to close the gap in deficiencies which some learners have and which keep them from being independent. Also, if the learner already possesses the behavioral change sought, then the instructional objectives are not necessary for him. Further, the learner's own purposes and desires may suggest important instructional outcomes.

A second source is the local, national, and world society which demands the teaching of customs, habits, and shared values which contribute to communication among peoples.

A third source is the disciplines, bodies of knowledge organized for effective inquiry, explanation, and teaching. Objectives drawn from this source give rise to theoretical ways for controlling the environment and propitiating man's spirit.

A fourth source is found in human activities such as government, agriculture, industry, and business whose skills, undertakings, and behaviors are presumed to contribute to the material prosperity of society. Objectives derived in response to this source are intended to support the existing institutions which carry on these essential activities. This support takes the form of the learner's (a) desire for the products from the institutions (popular consumption), (b) acceptance of procedures followed by the institution in discharging the activity (public relations), and (c) willingness to develop and give skills and talents necessary to the enterprise (vocational preparation and recruitment).

Each school, and to some extent each classroom, should consider formulating objectives drawn from these sources within the framework of the following major functions:

SUPPLEMENTING FUNCTION

This function arises directly out of the fact of individual differences. Before deciding what to teach, the school must note the mental, physical, and emotional characteristics of the intended learners. Differences among learners require two kinds of actions. Paradoxically, one action is intended to reduce differences and the other to increase differences.

First, there is the action of trying to bring all learners to a minimum level of performance in activities associated with "health, making a living, family life, social-civic activities, and recreation." Particularized objectives are necessary when, for instance, the secondary school finds that some enrollees have not acquired fundamental competencies such as those specified in *Elementary School Objectives*.[1] These supplemental objectives are chosen to close the gap between where the learner *is* and where it is desirable that he be with respect to these competencies.

The following are illustrations of supplemental objectives at the secondary school level.

Physical Development
a. States and recalls information of how infections are spread and the effects of alcohol and drugs on the body
b. Identifies weeds and plants and contents of packaged materials which may be poisonous
c. Demonstrates social skills through dancing, tennis, swimming, or other activities appropriate to his community and society

Ethical Behavior
a. States the laws and rules which he is expected to obey
b. Recognizes many similarities among racial, religious, and social groups
c. Disapproves of stealing and destroying the property of others

Social Relations and the Social World
a. Can introduce himself and others
b. Waits his turn in using equipment, being a leader, and so on

[1] Nolan C. Kearney, *Elementary School Objectives*. New York: Russell Sage Foundation, 1953.

c. States and illustrates some of the significant issues in international, political, social, and economic matters
d. Can read political, physiographical, and distribution maps
e. Able to illustrate formal "rules of order"

Physical World
a. Able to generalize in simple terms about seasonal changes; their effect upon the way people live, dress, and eat, and their effect upon plant and animal life
b. Has understandable answers to questions about sex and human reproduction
c. Applies criteria in distinguishing between fact and opinion in various kinds of physical situations

Aesthetic Development
a. Distinguishes effects of cool and warm colors, negative space
b. Recognizes rhythms that are similar
c. Able to count time and recognize measures, accent, and repeated rhythm patterns when listening to music
d. Identifies art objects consistent with principles of color, balance, and harmony
e. Explains the use of melody and harmony in simple recorded music
f. Able to read a simple melody, can reproduce with voice or instrument the music he can read

Communication
a. Able to find source materials in a wide variety of subjects, e.g., applies library skills
b. Distinguishes between literature that is plausible and that which misrepresents reality; distinguishes between literal and metaphorical language
c. Illustrates direct and indirect discourse; illustrates proper occasions for using formal and informal language
d. Has a reading comprehension vocabulary of at least 10,000 words and spells correctly the words he needs in writing
e. Can write paragraphs centered around a topic; can write correctly 9 out of 10 simple 5- to 10-word sentences
f. Can use an occasional compound or complex sentence
g. Adapts his voice and language usage to the audience and occasion
h. In simple reading, notes the sequence of ideas and identifies the author's outline
i. Describes the point of cartoons

Quantitative Relationship
a. Applies numbers to time, weight, dry and liquid measures
b. Measures to the nearest whole
c. Illustrates the place value of numerals and percentages
d. Shows the relationship of division to fractions (decimals)
e. Able to repeat all the fundamental combinations and to illustrate each of the four fundamental processes
f. Can compute simple interest with the aid of decimal fractions
g. Can read simple formulas such as those relating to the radius and circumference of a circle

Second, there is need for action to increase the differences among learners. We value variability, the extension of talent, and the right of the individual to become what he wants to become (provided this is not harmful to the group). Therefore, we must state objectives that will require developing individuals with special competencies.

Illustrations can be found in the writing of Spitznas[2] who tells of a fifth-grade boy who discoursed for hours on the subject of the Leni-Lenape Indians, their origins, their language, folkways, and customs, because this topic had fired his imagination and his enthusiasm. This boy does not differ in kind from the ninth-grade youngster in a general mathematics class who independently but with periodic supervision from his teacher went on to master the elements of first-year algebra. Nor does he differ from those elementary school children who are ready for instructional objectives calling for knowledge of chemical elements and compounds, atomic structure, formula writing, alloys, the action of gases, how to measure heat and light, and so on. Instructional objectives which include the application of advanced procedures and techniques of the arts in such fields as drama, journalism, and foreign language are in order.

INTEGRATING FUNCTION

Cultivation in the individual of those skills, knowledges, and dispositions minimally necessary for the common culture is the

[2] James E. Spitznas, "General, Special and Vocational Education: An Exploration of Distinctive Differences," *What Shall the High Schools Teach?* 1956 Yearbook, Washington, D.C.: Association for Supervision and Curriculum Development, 1956.

integrating function of the curriculum. A few years ago, seventy-five leading educators recommended a list of objectives believed appropriate for programs in general education. The recommendations of these educators[3] are the clearest statements we have about the integrating element in the educational program of the secondary school. Examples of the behavioral competencies sought are illustrated below:

Study Habits
a. Can read all parts of a newspaper for needed information
b. Can set up a procedure and carry it through for a project requiring work over a period of at least a week
c. Applies what he has learned to a new situation, e.g., setting up a job on a lathe in the machine shop
d. Applies a science principle to a personal health problem, a principle of grammar in a foreign language, the method of proof learned in geometry to the statement made in an advertisement

Communication
a. Writes social and business letters which are correct in form and clear in expression

Quantitative Thinking
a. Demonstrates that he can read and understand mathematical reports, charts, graphs, and simple statements of financial accounts

Logical Thinking
a. Able to identify flaws in purportedly logical discourse (e.g., circularity, *post hoc* attributions of cause, "undistributed middle") not by particular labels but simply as unwarranted claims of proof
b. Identifies unstated assumptions which are necessary to a line of argument

Citizenship
a. Recognizes why our civil liberties are indispensable; why a denial to one person or group increasingly results in similar denials to others
b. Shows willingness to defend the orderly process and place of law, and to work actively to get change where and when needed

[3] Will French and Associates, *Behavioral Goals of General Education in High School*. New York: Russell Sage Foundation, 1957.

c. Appraises ideas and action of nations in the light of differences in culture, physical factors, economic resources, and political conditions

Physical World

a. Sees the application of the basic principles of science to daily living, e.g., principles of heredity, laws of motion, activity of atoms and molecules, changes of matter and energy, origin and change in living things, basic ideas in anthropology

Values

a. Raises and discusses, on his own maturity level, ethical and moral questions as they have to do with community life and human welfare

b. Expresses in his behavior a value system that places the individual human personality high; applies this system both to his own and to other people's personalities

Aesthetic

a. Recognizes and applies principles of line, color, design and functional arrangement in many situations within his sphere of influence

Health

a. Is aware of the psychic needs which must be satisfied in order to have good health—the need for affection, belonging, recognition, and identification (something worth-while to live for)

b. Recognizes the danger signals of pain, fatigue, fever, then exercises judgment in self-medication, and obtains medical help when necessary

Economic

a. Recognizes the uses and abuses of the American profit system

b. Is able to compare and contrast major aspects of the different ways of organizing economic life, such as capitalism, communism, fascism, and socialism

c. Knows how the government and services of his community are financed and something of the economic structure of his community

Family

a. Understands something of the changing role of the family, American culture, and the problems faced by modern families as a result of social changes

Community Groups

a. Understands contributions of different ethnic groups to the American way of life and that the plurality of the cultures composing the community add richly to community life

Unresolved Issues

a. Familiar with issues surrounding the community's use, management, and conservation of the natural resources, e.g., opposes the commercialization of beauty spots
b. Is trying to develop informed opinions on the major issues of social and governmental policy at the national level, e.g., farm income, immigration, civil rights, natural resources, labor-capital, financing of public education
c. Makes discerning judgment on the reliability and completeness of information available in mass media
d. Recognizes and differentiates between legitimate and unwarranted pressure tactics to influence local, state, national, and world policy and action
e. Has some knowledge of employment restrictions, discrimination, opportunities, and protection imposed by or offered by trade unions, business organizations, professional associations, state examining boards, and legislations

EXPLORING AND SPECIALIZING FUNCTIONS

An exploratory function is being served when the school reveals to the pupil possibilities and opportunities which may warrant his subsequent choice of one or more fields for specialization. Out of incipient and tentative exposures to academic disciplines and to vocational experiences dealing with the major technological and commercial enterprises of the foreseeable future may come personal discoveries of genuine talent and ultimately, perhaps, devotion to inquiry in a discipline or zeal for developing technical competencies in a trade.

Specialization studies are those in which the current standards of the academic disciplines and trades prevail. Elementary and secondary schools have played down the specializing function, believing that it could best be discharged in post-high school years. The minimizing of this function left many youth without that feeling of personal worth which comes with knowledge that one is reasonably expert in some worthy field of endeavor. Currently, there are signs that a high degree of mastery in a discipline such as physics or an activity such as drafting will be among the general objectives for many youth while they are yet in the common school. The central arguments for offering the disciplines have been stated in Chapter III.

In exploring a discipline, the pupil should not be expected to master all the knowledge which the expert needs to possess. He should be expected to acquire basic knowledge of the field through which he can acquire further information as he desires. Also in his introduction the pupil will not be as precise as the specialist. If one is introduced to an item of knowledge at a general level, he will, over a period of time, make finer distinction until reaching a high level of precision.

Education in the disciplines is directed toward the more enduring learning of methods by which knowledge is derived, rather than to a terminal emphasis upon present states of knowledge. Under this proposition, the individual is not taught to recall the facts bearing on a necessary course of action in daily life; he is taught the notions and procedures necessary to acquire them. For instance, the method of historical research with its logic, values, and controls should be studied not to make children precocious historians but to show them how history is written.

General objectives for directing instruction in the disciplines often demand that the pupil:

a. Recalls references for specific verbal and nonverbal symbols in the discipline
b. Defines technical terms by giving their attributes, properties, or relations
c. Applies the criteria by which facts, principles, opinions, and conduct in the field are tested or judged
d. States the methods of attack relevant to the kinds of problems of concern to the discipline
e. States the important principles and generalizations by which a complex phenomenon, problem, or the discipline itself is viewed.

Sometimes high-level objectives are proposed which call for the synthesis of knowledge:

a. Proposes ways of testing hypotheses
b. Perceives various possible ways in which experience may be organized to form a conceptual structure
c. Formulates appropriate hypotheses based upon an analysis of factors involved, and modifies such hypotheses in the light of new factors and considerations.

The school should refer to curriculum materials prepared by the academic disciplines as they formulate objectives in exploration and specialization. A description of these materials and ways to obtain them is found in *Using Current Curriculum Developments*.[4]

Illustrations of objectives typical to the disciplinary approach are listed below for physics and geography. The reader will note that these objectives are consistent with the assumption that instruction in the disciplines involves (a) understanding of a common core of subject matter, by no means merely encyclopedic in nature, and (b) development of skill in the methodology or process employed by the scientist in exploring the universe about him. He will also note that the objectives provide for both subject matter and behavior.

PHYSICS

On page 58 is a matrix for ensuring that evidence is collected with respect to all important instructional objectives. Only those squares of the chart which represent the particular objectives sought need be marked. If, for example, a student were expected to be able to use graphic presentation of data in connection with measurement and diffraction of light, the appropriate square would be marked and specific tasks would be set up to reveal the student's attainment of this objective.

GEOGRAPHY

a. *Location*. Location is the linchpin of geography. Ideally, by the end of his course, the student of geography will display a love for maps and a curiosity for knowing where places are. His knowl-

[4] Association for Supervision and Curriculum Development, *Using Current Curriculum Developments*. Washington, D.C.: National Education Association, 1963.

SUBJECT MATTER	Ability to demonstrate qualitative understanding of fundamentals	Ability to apply knowledge to unfamiliar situations	Ability to analyze problems, situations mathematically	Ability to use graphical presentation of data	Ability to identify problems in a new situation	Ability to formulate a simple scientific model	Ability to make logical predictions based on a model	Ability to make relevant observations	Ability to suggest new lines of investigation based on observation	Ability to draw valid conclusions from observations and data	TOTALS
Time											
Space											
Motion											
Mass											
Matter											
Measurement											
Behavior of light											
Geometric optics											
Wave motion											
Interference and diffraction of light											
Force											
Momentum											
Conservation of momentum											
Kinetic and potential energy											
Magnetic fields											
Photons and matter waves											
Quantum systems											
TOTALS											

* F. L. Ferris, "Testing for Physics Achievement," *American Journal of Physics,* Vol. 28, March 1960, p. 269.

edge of facts about places will be inextricably tied to the location of these places, and when he learns any significant thing about a place he should be uneasy until he has "looked up" the location of the place if he does not already know it; in other words, he will have formed the "atlas habit" just as the student of English forms the "dictionary habit."

b. *Map Reading.* One of the most distinctive traits of a geographer is his ability to read and understand maps, and the student of geography should be trained in this skill, for without it he will experience considerable difficulty in all other phases of geography. The general ability of relating the map to the earth has five principal aspects:

1) The student should understand the standard point, line, and area *symbols* which are used to represent qualitative and quantitative distributions, and he should be able to extract information from maps which use these symbols. He should also be able to visualize the *terrain* of an area by studying maps that use various standard techniques of terrain representation.

2) The relationship between distances on the earth and distances on the map, or the *scale* of the map, can vary tremendously; the student should know how to determine the scale of a map and he should be able to judge the kinds of information which are most likely to be shown or omitted at various scales.

3) The student should be able to determine *direction* on a map, whatever its orientation, for he should realize that no map orientation is better than any other, despite the traditional orientation of maps with north at the top.

4) The student should be able to use systems of map *coordinates,* such as latitude and longitude, or township and range, to locate and identify places on the map.

5) The student should be skilled at mentally correcting for the distortion inevitably associated with map *projections* used in representing the round earth on flat paper.

c. *Content of Areas.* The student should possess detailed factual information about specific parts of the world, but differences in course organization make it impossible to specify the areas, or even types of areas, for which he should have such information. An ingenious method of testing his knowledge is to present him with a description of an area from which all names have been deleted, and to ask him where he believes the area is, and his reasons for this belief.

d. *Production of Creative Geography.* Within set limits, the student should be able to demonstrate that he can do the things that geographers do. The four stages of geographic investigation at which he might be expected to demonstrate a certain degree of proficiency are:

1) the ability to *observe* significant differences and relationships out of doors in his own home area, and to *record* these observations accurately.

2) the ability to *prepare accurate maps* from his own field observations and from other sources and to examine these maps for significant relationships.

3) the ability to *describe* an *area* in which he has worked or about which he has gathered information, making use of the standard conventions, criteria of selection, and vocabulary of geographers.

4) the ability to *formulate* geographic *hypotheses* and to test these hypotheses in the light of data he is able to obtain. Ideally, he should use mathematical tools for this purpose, for the use of mathematical tools in solving geographic problems is one of the important frontiers of current research in geography, but so far the results of this research have been presented mainly in forms unsuited to introduction into the educational program.[5]

Statement of Philosophy

In the final analysis, the question of what to teach is a matter of value itself. Any board of education and faculty would do well to

[5] Association of American Geographers and the National Council for Geographic Education, "Advisory Paper for Teachers Associated with the High School Geography Project," William D. Pattison, Project Director, 1962.

examine their stated objectives in the light of a number of assumptions such as those appearing below. These assumptions will help determine alternatives which should not be taught in school. A good school is known by what it refuses to teach as well as by what it does teach.

1) Is it something for which no other agency other than the school can or should be responsible?

2) Is it economical in terms of the resources of the school?

3) Is it something that the child will not acquire without systematic and deliberate instruction?

4) Will it facilitate learning in later grades?

5) Will it enable the learner to use his experiences outside the school in a more educative fashion?

6) Will it increase the student's ability to generate new hypotheses and to conceptualize alternatives and their consequences?

7) Does it permit a child to overcome the limitations of his home environment and allow him to live a different life from that of his parents? (For example, does it permit the offering of college preparatory programs to pupils whose predecessors have always gone directly into the labor force following graduation from high school?)

8) Does it allow him to question existing institutions in the light of larger values, such as Bill of Rights, and the Universal Declaration of Human Rights?

9) Is it relevant to conditions of life in the foreseeable future rather than part of a tradition that is obsolete in the light of changed conditions?

Additional Readings

Bloom, Benjamin S., ed., *Taxonomy of Educational Objectives*. New York: Longmans, Green and Company, 1956.

Fraser, Dorothy M., *Deciding What To Teach*. Washington, D.C.: National Education Association, 1963.

French, Will and Associates, *Behavioral Goals of General Education in High School.* New York: Russell Sage Foundation, 1957.

Kearney, Nolan C., *Elementary School Objectives.* New York: Russell Sage Foundation, 1953.

Mager, Robert F., *Preparing Objectives for Programed Instruction.* San Francisco: Fearon Publishers, 1961.

Using Current Curriculum Developments. Washington, D.C.: Association for Supervision and Curriculum Development, National Education Association, 1963. A report of national projects which have answered the questions of what to teach in the fields of the arts, English, foreign language, health education and physical education, mathematics, science, social studies, and vocational and technical education.

PART III. LEARNING OPPORTUNITIES AND THEIR ORGANIZATION

THERE IS A woeful unawareness of the principles for the selection of learning opportunities. In fact, textbooks, films, language laboratories, teachers, and excursions are often not even seen as learning opportunities leading to particular objectives. Instead, too often, they are regarded as ends rather than means. Content and devices are introduced without consideration of the particular learners and the instructional objectives.

Further, the ordering of the opportunities selected and the responses they are to elicit has been carried out in a haphazard and piecemeal fashion, contrary to a primary purpose of formal schooling, namely, systematic instruction. Systematic organization is the great unfinished task of American schools.

Chapter 5 establishes principles for the systematic organization of subject matter in light of objectives and learners and illustrates these principles in concrete instances. The importance of an organizational element is made vividly clear in this chapter. Frequent failure to recognize such an element is responsible for discontinuity in learning and stunting of the learners' growth.

Chapter 6 continues with the discussion by showing the centrality of principles for selection of learning opportunities if schooling is to be educative. Without application of these principles, it is doubtful that administrators can contribute much to improving instruction, and certainly teachers who do not apply these principles in arranging classroom interactions are unlikely to succeed in the attainment of instructional objectives.

V. Patterns of Curriculum Organization

EVERY SCHOOL has its immediate curriculum problem in deciding how best to attain the objectives of instruction. Some administrators abdicate this responsibility. They never ask:

"Is it possible that many of our learners can acquire the desired competencies in a class that meets only three days a week instead of daily?"

"When will thirty-minute periods be more effective than periods of two hours?"

"What objectives require several years of continous instruction?"

"Would it make any practical difference if social studies were not offered in the primary grades?

"Under what conditions would the scheduling of lectures before large numbers of students be more instructionally effective than small-group discussion?"

Instead, too many administrators avoid these problems by (a) appealing to a checklist like those in the Conant report (e.g., "the time devoted to English composition during the four years should occupy about half the total time devoted to the study of English"), to college recommendations (e.g., "two years of a laboratory science is recommended"), or to mandated requirements by the State Department of Education (e.g., "five years of instruction in the use of English and history are required.") and

(b) merely blocking out time in the school day when pupils are to be directed in something called "reading," "English," "history," and the like. The relation between these topics or subjects and instructional objectives is infrequently taken into account. Furthermore, the relationship between instructional variables like classroom activities, methods of instruction, frequency and length of meeting, as well as composition and size of class are seldom tied to instructional objectives and to the particular learners concerned.

Although the State by statute and directives and colleges and universities by admission requirements have determined parts of the curriculum, they have usually done so in very general terms, leaving details to the schools. Moreover, there is much room for interpretation of these requirements. Deviations by individual administrators and teachers are in order. The point to make here is that too often there is a confusion of means with ends. If administrators and teachers select and organize details of knowledge and activities in terms of desired attitudes, habits, and intellectual patterns of action, the program promises more effective returns. An organized curriculum should keep before pupils and teachers alike the real ends of education and the relation of all details to them.

Administration of the curriculum is nonintellectual when there is no conscious recognition of the relationship between means and ends and when there is no exercising of judgment about the ends of instruction. By way of illustration, a school sometimes introduces a detail of instruction such as a foreign language laboratory (i.e., taped lesson calling for practice in pronunciation) without recognizing that this instructional tool will determine to a great extent the instructional objective for a language program. The language laboratory shifts the objective from ability to read a foreign language and to explain aspects of a foreign culture to ability to demonstrate verbal fluency (correct pronunciation) in street-level conversations. The *intellectual* administrator introduces the language laboratory because he has decided that verbal fluency is the outcome sought and because he has weighed its desirability against other possible instructional outcomes. The *nonintellectual* administrator "buys" the language laboratory without weighing its instructional consequences in terms of a range of possible instructional outcomes. He is a technician or opportunist who has permitted the producer and distributor of the artifact to determine the instructional outcomes for the language program.

The selection of details of instruction (e.g., textbooks, teachers, instructional devices, units, projects, methods, and tests) is so important that we have devoted the next chapter to principles and illustrations for conducting this curriculum task. The present chapter will deal with principles and arrangements for organizing details of instruction so that the desired competencies develop in learners.

Criteria Used by Administrators in Evaluating Curriculum Organization

Administrators assume that the curricular organization of a school or program is good if it meets these criteria:

a. There is stipulation of courses or activities required of all pupils.

b. There is stipulation of courses or activities available to pupils with particular interests and abilities.

c. The length of class periods is adequate to the instructional objectives.

d. Electives are available in varying time allotments.

e. There is a sequence of courses in a field.

f. There is coordination of instructional activities with different grade levels.

g. There is coordination of instructional activities in one area with other areas in the same grade level.

h. There is provision for pupil participation in related activities outside the school building.

i. Cyclical arrangements (alternating between semesters or years) are followed when enrollments are small.

j. Remedial or clinical activities are available in addition to instruction in regular courses.

k. Grade lines are minimized by placing pupils in groups based on their level of ability and interests.

l. Courses are organized by themes, problems, topics, and projects.

m. Attention is given in planning programs to avoid long gaps between the end of study (e.g., foreign language) in school and the beginning of the same study in college.

n. There is provision for use of facilities during free periods, after school, or on Saturdays.

o. Courses are organized into a few comprehensive units built around key concepts and fundamental precepts.

p. Curriculum plans provide for repetition and needed review of important ideas but avoidance in duplication of experiences.

q. There is provision for discontinuance of activities found to be ineffective.

The Essence of Good Curriculum Organization and the Problem of Organization

Determining organization of learning experiences poses these questions:

How can the learning experiences of next week and next month best reinforce those of this week and this month so as to produce a maximum cumulative effect?

How can the learning experiences of this semester not only reinforce those of last semester but go more deeply and more broadly into the field so as to get increasingly deeper and broader understandings on the part of students?

How can the learning experiences in English (or any other field) be related to those in social studies (or any other field) so that appropriate and efficient reinforcement may be provided?[1]

A good curriculum organization meets three specifications: (a) There is planning for review and reiteration of that which has been learned (skill, concept, value). This is called meeting the criterion of *continuity*. (b) In addition to providing for practice of an important learning, the curriculum must extend that learning in depth. Planning for such an extension is called meeting the criterion of *sequence*. An example of sequence has been given in which the word "intuition" is first regarded in the sense of a femi-

[1] Ralph W. Tyler, *Toward Improved Curriculum Theory*, "The Organization of Learning Experiences," Supplementary Educational Monograph No. 71. Chicago: The University of Chicago Press, 1950, p. 60.

nine foreboding; next, in the sense of tuition, including notions of teaching and the cost of instruction; later the term is considered from its Latin roots "to watch, to guard, to protect"; and so on until the learner generalizes the term into a question such as whether or not humans can acquire knowledge other than through sense experience. (c) The skills, values, and concepts taught in one area of study should be related to the other areas of study and problems of life. In these ways the learnings are "kept alive" and there is a better chance for obtaining transfer (the ability to apply a learning in new situations). When one plans for this, he has met the criterion of *integration,* the correlation of subject matter.

Central to continuity, sequence, and integration is identification of those elements which are to be reiterated (continued), deepened (sequenced), and broadened (integrated). By looking at instructional objectives, one finds the content and activity which serve as these elements. The element in its various forms, components, aspects, and prerequisites is that which is reviewed, ordered, and cumulated. Let us illustrate the relationship of an element in an instructional objective to its appearance in a plan of organization. The hypothetical objective is *the learner is able to look at a clock and tell the hour to the nearest minute.* The element of content is the concept of hour and minute; the element of behavior is that which the learner is to do with the concept. An analysis of this objective might include the importance of a child's being able (a) to count to 60, (b) to relate numbers to numerals, (c) to demonstrate the ratio of numbers to hours, (d) to recognize the significance of big and little "hands" and big and little numbers, and (e) to be able to respond to the notion of "clockwise." For each of these sub-objectives there would be many learning opportunities or experiences in which the child would learn to notice differentiations. He would get practice in making correct discriminations and responses necessary to performance in the subobjectives. Organization would be the ordering of these opportunities so that they cumulate in the ability to read a clock to the nearest hour and minute.

The heart of the organizational problem is being clear about the instructional objective and identification of the steps necessary to its attainment. Subsidiary questions involve how best to order these steps for effective learning.

An illustration of the organizing principle "simple to complex" is shown in Gorelick's typology of curriculum objectives for the mentally retarded:

waits in line for a drink without pushing others > takes turns > shows good manners > is able to get along with others

takes one crayon > responds to the concept of one > responds to number concepts up to five > responds to number concepts

discriminates between initial consonant *b* and *s* > discriminates between initial consonants > is able to use word attack skills > is able to read.[2]

Unfortunately, curriculum inquiry has not advanced to the place where we know what constitute necessary steps in the attainment of objectives. Many so-called prerequisites are just so much busy work. A case in point is a reading readiness workbook which elicits only gross discriminations of "like" and "unlike." The importance of giving a child many types of sensory experiences is sometimes used to justify just about any activity in the primary grades, whether or not it is logically related to the instructional task for which the activity is to "ready" the child. There is little likelihood that many of these experiences will be associated in the child's mind with the task of learning, say, numbers and forms in mathematics, reading, and science unless the school arranges conditions to show this relevancy directly to the child.

Learning Theory and Curriculum Organization

Current plans for reorganization of the curriculum, from kindergarten upward, are among the boldest attempts at curriculum improvement ever attempted. In mathematics, for instance, there are deliberate efforts to develop programs within 20 or 30 years so that virtually all sixth-grade students will attain a level of mathematical competencies well above that of the general population today, and at the completion of high school these students will have attained a level "comparable to three years of top-level college

[2] Molly C. Gorelick, "A Typology of Curriculum Objectives for Mentally Retarded: from Ambiguity to Precision," *Mental Retardation,* August 1963.

training today" with the equivalent of two years of calculus and one semester each of modern algebra and probability theory. These plans are undertaken on the psychological assumption "that any subject can be taught effectively in some intellectually honest form to any child at any stage of development."[3] The first essential is to identify the "subject," the "basic concepts" or the "underlying principles" which will enable the learner to see the connection between things.

To take an example from mathematics, algebra is a way of arranging knowns and unknowns in equations so that the unknowns are made knowable. The three fundamentals involved in working with these equations are commutation, distribution, and association. Once a student grasps the ideas embodied by these three fundamentals, he is in a position to recognize wherein "new" equations to be solved are not new at all, but variants on a familiar theme.[4]

The second essential is to cast these key ideas or operations, e.g., commutation, distribution, and association, in forms that are within the intellectual reach of children of different ages.

An example of this has been reported by Keislar who describes a way of teaching first-grade children to learn mathematics in terms of algebraic structures. Cuisenaire blocks (colored blocks of different lengths) to represent algebraic quantities were used. Children at the beginning manipulated the blocks without reference to number. Later, the same problems were presented with numbers placed on the blocks corresponding to the length of the block in centimeters. The children responded primarily to length and number. Later, the learner was shown the numbers alone and was required to answer without the use of blocks. The only concrete illustration given of the principles and arithmetical relationships consisted of the lengths of the blocks. Children learned to find for themselves the sum of two numbers; they learned this presumably by manipulating blocks that were labeled with certain numbers. The symbols "plus," "minus," "greater than," and "smaller than" and equality and multiplication signs were introduced entirely with

[3] Jerome S. Bruner, *The Process of Education*. Cambridge: Harvard University Press, 1961, p. 33.
[4] *Ibid.*, p. 7.

reference to block manipulation. At the end of 15 weeks, pupils were given plastic symbols of numbers and letters in various combinations and asked to build as many true mathematical statements as they could. They also were required to rewrite algebraic statements in a different form in which only the letters were to be inserted. (e.g., $T - H = U$ was to be commuted in a box that appeared as follows: $(\quad - \quad = \quad)$[5]

The point of all this is to reiterate the notion that what is taught in the lower grades should be related to that which is to come. Development of powerful ideas takes much time and requires systematic instruction. It is the business of the school to organize materials that will make the development of these ideas possible. A good curriculum organization allows the teacher to take the long look ahead. We have not been very successful in systematically organizing our instruction. We have not always identified the elements (abstractions, powerful concepts, values, or skills) to be extended and we have not shown how these elements would appear at different times in the life of the children in order to be meaningful.

At the present our assumptions about learning seem to suggest that there are three stages in the intellectual development of a child which require differentiated treatment of the element. Before an approximate mental age of five, the child manipulates the element through action. During the approximate ages six to thirteen, the child manipulates the symbols that represent concrete elements and their relations. Later, the child engages in "as if" behavior, developing new propositions with the element, deducing new relationships which have not been previously experienced.

A much older theory of learning with implications for organization is the belief that the learning processes of children follow the same pattern as the learning process of the race (cultural-epoch hypothesis). Modern educators in the United States thought this view naive and rejected it as a theory for learning. Currently, however, a considerable number of American music teachers are

[5] Evan R. Keislar, "Teaching Science and Mathematics by Auto-instruction in the Primary Grades: An Experimental Strategy in Curriculum Development," in John E. Coulson, ed., *Programmed Learning and Computer-Based Instruction*. New York: John Wiley and Sons, Inc., 1962, pp. 99–112.

showing an interest in curriculum developed on such an assumption.

Orff started his *Musik fur Kinder* experiment in the 1930's. . . . Primitive man has used free bodily movement in dance and also simple rhythmic drum patterns, and so Orff began with drums suited to the children's physical size and skill, combining bodily movements with the beat of the drum. He also added rhythmic chants, synchronizing the spoken rhythm with the other movements.

Next came melodic experimentation. Many primitive peoples' first musical utterances employ only one or two pitches, and perhaps finally progress to the use of the five-tone scale. Using this same sequence, Orff started the musical experiences planned for little folks by writing songs with only two or three notes and, at the most, five notes from the pentatonic scale. He expanded the melodic vocabulary to include other steps only after the children had had a great deal of experience with the very simple melodies.[6]

We can accept Orff's plan for ordering learning experiences connecting the element "musicality," e.g., rhythm and melody, without accepting the theory that mental development repeats the culture of the human race. In fact, we could say that Orff was merely following the organizing principle of going "from the simple to the complex."

A number of such organizing principles about how experiences at one point in time can best be related to those at another point have been proposed. These principles sometimes state that it is more effective to begin with the familiar and move to the unfamiliar, from the seen (practical) to the unseen (theoretical), from the concrete to the abstract. An idea which subsumes more ideas than another is said to be more abstract; the abstract idea allows one to handle more particulars. As indicated in Chapter 3, these principles should not be applied without consideration of the instructional objectives. Some objectives call for the observation-and analysis of individuals and the envolvement of general laws and truths. Other objectives demand the application of broad general-

[6] Marguerite V. Hood, "The Music Education Curriculum—Recent Developments and Experimentation," in Paul C. Rosenbloom, ed., *Modern Viewpoints in the Curriculum.* New York: McGraw-Hill Book Co., 1964, p. 109.

izations to specific instances believed best fostered by procedures in which there is division toward particulars. A combination of both is usually wanted. In its concern for going from (a) sensory experiences (particulars) to more abstract thinking (universals) and (b) powerful abstractions to new sensory experiences (particulars), schools have not recognized that the transition from abstract to particular or concrete is as difficult as going from concrete to abstract.

At present, we have little agreement about the best organizing principles for attainment of particular objectives. Within the field of mathematics, for instance, most argue that the acquisition of mathematical concepts occurs best following many concrete experiences with objects of varied size and number from which the child is led to abstract various notions of number and quantity. However, as in Keislar's study, there is a case for the elimination of concrete illustrations in which extraneous factors may distract the learner from the abstract relationships to be learned. A related issue is that which asks "When should learners be asked to verbalize or name the concept he is using?" Materials organized by the University of Illinois Committee on School Mathematics delay verbalization; other programs call for immediate verbalization of the principle, possibly on the assumption that the language itself can help the learner mediate between known instances and unfamiliar instances of the same class of events.

We must select organizing principles that match instructional objectives. Suppose a teacher of history has an instructional objective that calls for the identification of those current social events which are consistent with or inconsistent with the Bill of Rights. Should he organize his course in accordance with the principle of *chronology,* arranging experiences dealing with historical events as they occurred in time, or should he arrange experiences in accordance with the principle of *increasing the breadth of application?* On the other hand, if his objective calls for pupils' recalling historical events as a consecutive narrative, would he not find the chronological plan more appropriate?

Results of psychological experiments in the mass media are giving some direction for educators in deciding how best to order experiences for particular learners and objectives. If one were interested in developing learners who would resist an ideological view contrary to those prevalent in the community, he probably would begin with one-sided arguments and only present both viewpoints to older students. On the other hand, while one-sided arguments are quite effective with those already convinced, two-sided arguments are necessary to innoculate students against the effects of countercommunications and to strengthen the appeal by presenting well-known facts on the other side.

Schools have arranged learning opportunities in accordance with presumed interests, psychological problems, and social demands of children. These tend to follow the principles of *geographic extension, broader range of contacts,* and *usefulness.* Because beginners in school were presumed to be interested in the home, planned experiences in the kindergarten dealt with home life; later, experiences were ordered to parallel the child's expanding interest in school, community, state, nation, and world. There is a paradox in this procedure. One is interested in that for which he has been rewarded, therefore, he will be taught that for which he has been rewarded. When psychology began to see "interests" as the result of cultural and personal reinforcement (reward) rather than "innate" manifestations, educators began to see that children could be as "interested" in far-off places as they were in the near at hand. If a mother who is important in the eyes of the child consistently praises the child when he approximates some behavior related to China, that child will soon be interested in China.

With respect to the placement of experiences dealing with personal problems, curriculum organizers must again ask "What are the instructional objectives?" If it is important for the learner to intellectually understand the underlying causes of personal problems faced and consequences of actions taken by teenagers and to treat these problems objectively, it might be better to introduce such problems for study to pre-teens before the pupil is likely to become emotionally involved or before they are his problems.

On the other hand, it is often desirable to introduce content at the same time that the learner has a use for this content in his daily life. For instance, principles of health and safety might well appear at the very time these principles are to be acted upon in life outside of school. The latter procedure is, of course, an instance of integration or correlation.

We do not have principles for bringing about integration of subject matter as we do the sequencing of subject matter. The psychology for the relating of concepts has been less fully explored than that for the formulating of concepts. What little data we do have show that two kinds of problems must be met. First, there is the problem of differentiating separate concepts. This includes avoiding the confusion caused by generalizing from objects and events on the basis of unessential features. It also means paying attention to the difference between terms and the things for which they stand. For example, realism in literature and in philosophy does not have the same referrents.

The other problem is the bringing together of separate concepts in an effort to permit the student to see problems and objects in their different connections. A case in point is the attempt to apply a concept in a practical problem-solving situation. When one has to apply a complex particular "lifelike" method of work which he has acquired through copying in a formal "school-like" situation, he will fail unless he has learned to use the principle underlying the method and to identify the relevant different variables present in the new situation.

Organizing Structures

Structure has been defined as the way in which instructional time of the school is divided so as to provide a series of periods in which learning experiences are set up and organized. Structures common to schools are (1) program of studies, (2) curriculum in a field, e.g., science curriculum, (3) course of study, (4) unit, and (5) lesson plan.

A *program of studies* consists of all offerings in the school or school system. These offerings may be specified as school subjects (disciplines), activities, problems, or skills for acquiring knowledge and habits. A curriculum in a field is a lengthy ordering of learning experiences in a particular domain of knowledge, e.g., science, humanities, social sciences, mathematics, and applied fields (business, industrial arts, and home economics). A *curriculum* in mathematics, for instance, may be twelve years in length. A *course of study* is composed of learning experiences in a field or problem area ordered for a semester or year. In the elementary school the course of study is often undifferentiated with respect to areas of knowledge. The elementary school teacher gives emphasis to habits for the acquisition of knowledge, e.g., reading, writing, and arithmetic, and specific behaviors consistent with moral and social values, e.g., applauds the courageous efforts of others. A *unit* is a series of learning experiences which culminate in the resolvement of a problem or task. A course of study is often composed of several units. A *lesson plan* is the arrangement for ordering of instruction for a single period.

A program of study arranged for a small high school (500 students) is excerpted below:

9th Grade	10th Grade	11th Grade	12th Grade
Algebra 1, 2 General Math	Geometry	Algebra 3, 4	Senior Math Math Analysis
Social Studies	Social Studies	Social Studies	Social Studies
English	English	English	Composition Literature
PE and Health	PE and Health	PE and Health	PE and Health
Foreign Lang.	Foreign Lang.	Foreign Lang.	Foreign Lang.
Science	Biology	Chemistry	Physics
	World of Art	Art Design Ceramics	Life Drawing Painting
		Music History	Music Harmony
Homemaking	Homemaking: Foods Personal Arts 1, 2	Homemaking: Clothing Child Care 3, 4	Homemaking: Home Living 5, 6
Industrial Arts	Industrial Arts	Industrial Arts	Industrial Arts
	Typing 1, 2	Shorthand 1, 2	Shorthand 3, 4

Activities: Choral, Instrumental Music, Council, Remedial Reading, Reading Improvement, Drama, Speech, Typing, Journalism, Driver Training, etc.

The program of studies illustrated above is formulated on the assumption (a) that integrating and exploring functions would be chiefly met through courses required by all, e.g., English three years; (b) that supplemental functions would be strengthened through an activities curriculum featuring offerings or projects such as remedial reading and science fairs, and (c) that the specializing function is met when a student completes a major, continuous work in one field for four years. The title of the courses or activities gives only general direction to the content to be introduced and to the objectives to be sought. In the example provided, "Social Studies" could mean a course organized as a separate discipline like "History" in which powers of explanation and inquiry would be the desired outcome. When taught as a discipline, the course would be organized in accordance with the subject-matter theory of organization. Social Studies could also be called "Problems of Democracy" in which important social problems would be considered in relation to not only the pertinent facts (descriptive knowledge, or *what is*) but especially in relation to the values involved (prescriptive knowledge, or what *should be*). If it were this kind of problems course, the outcome would be the development of practical intelligence.[7] One shows he has such intelligence when he can face an unresolved social situation and make a decision about it. This calls for assessing the fitness of the decision and a commitment to undertake a certain course of action. When taught as a course for decision-making and commitment, a social studies course is organized in accordance with the *core curriculum theory of organization*.

In a core curriculum pattern of organization, one does not merely decide whether conclusions about a situation follow logically from a set of facts and premises; he expresses a preference after surveying values and decides whether he is prepared to do something in practice about the issue under consideration. "Social Studies" can also be organized in accordance with an *activity theory of curriculum organization*. "Student Government" could be an instance of such an activity, in which the interests of students (e.g., how to get more school dances) serve as the target and

---

[7] R. Bruce Raup *et al.*, *The Improvement of Practical Intelligence*. New York: Harper & Brothers, 1950.

instructional content; knowledge, values, and habits are acquired in its pursuit. In the illustration of a program of study, "Student Government" would be a social studies offering and most likely be placed within an activity period.

Organizing Centers

An organizing center is the theme, topic, problem, or project which gives immediate purpose and direction to the undertaking of a number of learning experiences. The popularity of an organizing center stems from the assumption that learning best occurs when the learner is confronted with a problematic situation. In the resolvement of the problem, relevant information, methods, and details acquire significance. Further, the tension generated by the problem is believed to "motivate" the learner.

Within subject-matter courses such as "Physics" and "Linguistics," we find such organizing centers as the following: *matter, light, motion; sentence-modifiers, semantics,* and *morphology.* Core courses such as "Problems of Democracy" and "Finding Values by which to Live" are likely to develop units around such centers as: *How should we zone our community? Conservation and the improvement of daily living, The meaning of justice, The problem of evil.* Activity programs in the "Social Studies" at the primary level and "Student Government" and "Personal Psychology" on the secondary level might have units predicated on interests of pupils, such as *the airport, the newspaper, what should we do about school clubs?* and *how to establish personal relations with those of own and other sex.*

Relation of Organizing Centers to Organizing Elements

The use of organizing centers as focal points for ordering learning experiences has caused confusion. Parents and pupils alike think that the teacher is teaching *light, conservation, Africa* and a host of other topics and activities. This is only a partial truth. Much information and methodology related to the center are presented. However, this information and the resolvement of

Examples of Relations in Organizational Structure

ORGANIZATIONAL ELEMENT: ENERGY (other elements would be "life," "matter")	ELEMENTARY SCHOOL Science Program	SECONDARY SCHOOL			CURRICULUM IN SCIENCE showing only one organizational element "energy"
		Physics	Chemistry	Biology	
	Muscular forces, e.g., pulling, pushing, lifting various objects as examples of exerting a force	Energy— electrical and atomic structure	Chemical reaction and energy, e.g., energy liberated or consumed, qualitative ideas of energy "humps"	Functions of living organisms in terms of physical and chemical concepts of energy, experiments or responses of roots and stems to gravity, changes in muscular energy	
	Work and energy	Energies associated with loss and gain of electrons			
	Elastic forces	Etc.	Energy associated with bond formation and rupture	Receptors and relating stimuli to forms of energy	
	Friction-gravity				
	Energy of motion		Etc.	Etc.	
	Mechanical energy				
	Heat				
	Etc.				

	Concept of Organism	Principles of Reproduction	Ecological Principles	Genetics	Natural Selection	Course of Study: BIOLOGY
ENERGY	Changes in muscular energy, e.g., energy of position, of motion, of heat	Movement against gravity Embryology, regulation of differentiations	Interrelation of organism and environment	Mechanisms of gene action	....	

Unit: CONCEPT OF ORGANISM

	Concept of Organism
ENERGY	Organization Metabolism Regulatory Mechanisms

the problem or completion of the project are not the ends of instruction. The real instructional objectives (what is taught) are the behavioral changes the teacher is trying to effect by means of the centers. The learning experiences presented within a unit should be instances of the organizational elements (key abstractions or skills) which will culminate in the desired behavioral changes specified in the objectives. The organizing center is but a convenient way to bring concreteness and an immediate sense of unity and coherence to a number of learning experiences.

A simple illustration may help make this point. Teachers in primary grades frequently find that children have problems in the area of human relations (e.g., how to express affection to parents or friends). An immediate answer to this problem often takes the form of a tangible project, e.g., the making of a gift, the writing of a letter. Although the project has inherent value for the learner, its instructional value is determined by the extent to which it contributes to instructional objectives such as *able to attach sound and meaning to words in written language, able to use books for information and recreation.* In the writing of a letter, there would be many opportunities for formulating the abstraction relevant to the objective, e.g., *able to apply word attack skills.*

Similar confusion exists in connection with courses of study. To assume that "Physics" or "Ceramics" is what one learns is nonsense. It is the organizational elements of these fields which serve as the ultimate outcomes of knowledge in the subject. Furthermore, without instructional elements and objectives there is no way to relate the various organizing structures to each other. As shown in the diagram on pages 80 and 81, the unit is related to the course of study and the course of study to the curriculum.

Organizing Patterns and Functions of Curriculum

Earlier we said that objectives consistent with particular functions might best be attained through special patterns of organization. The activity pattern is characterized by (a) selection of activities (projects and problems) of interest and concern to a given sample of learners, and the correlate (b) preparation of resource materials which have been found to be useful in dealing with interests and problems among the population of learners from which the present sample is to be drawn.

It is logical to assume that objectives formulated on the basis of purposes and deficiencies of particular learners can best be considered in a curriculum pattern which does not call for specifying objectives before the arrival of the pupils and which permits the activities of interest to these pupils to serve as the organizing centers for learning experiences.

If a number of pupils are found to have serious defects in their physical posture, an activity curriculum in corrective physical education would be ordered. Here, each child would have his own objective. In addition to the advantage it offers the teacher wanting to adapt to the learners' deficiencies, the activity curriculum allows more flexibility in the selection of experiences to fulfill individual talents. The pupil with talents in poetry or reporting may profit from such activities as the publishing of a newspaper or literary magazine, activities which would be less likely to be the center for organization under core and subject-matter patterns.

Although the activity curriculum provides opportunity for the learner to explore, to get an indication as to whether he has the talent or zeal for certain kinds of tasks, we believe that the exploring function can best be discharged within the framework of the subject-matter curriculum (disciplines), in which the knowledge necessary for success in a range of activities is made available. Certainly, the specializing function, including the power of explanation and *inquiry,* is best met within a disciplined pattern in which topics and questions of great import to participants in the realm are the organizing centers.

The attainment of instructional objectives derived in response to crucial issues facing society is the integrating responsibility of schools. The cultivation of common outlooks, skills, and dispositions necessary for a united culture is consistent with the principles of a core curriculum. It is important to note that the core curriculum does not have correlation as its distinctive feature. Correlation, the selecting of a number of subjects around a central study, may indeed take place, but the essence of the core is to provide basic grounds and purposes upon which the minds and actions of all members of the community can meet. The organizing centers of the core curriculum are instances of the issues and social problems which have not been resolved.

Current theory of curriculum organization has modified the older notion of concentration. An elementary school teacher and her class may still absorb themselves in problems or projects such as *How shall we zone our community?* or *The newspaper* or *Japan.* In dealing with these topics, information from a variety of subjects is brought to bear. However, unless there is an identified organizing element in this activity, the instructional plan does not meet the standards of a good curriculum. The instructional objectives for these problems or projects might be: *able to illustrate the issue of government versus individual freedom* or *ability to distinguish facts from hypotheses.* The notion of government versus individual freedom and the skill of distinguishing facts from hypotheses could be the organizational elements leading toward these objectives. The content of the organizational elements has wide applicability and would be appropriate for learners anywhere. The problem or project selected may be temporal or parochial in nature, of immediate value to a select group of learners.

Nuclear and Cortical Organization of Curriculum

In 1961 the National Education Association and the Project on the Instructional Program of the Public Schools arranged for a Disciplines Seminar at which many knowledgeable scholars and scientists met with leading teachers and others concerned with education in schools. The seminar was called to facilitate study and effective use of the disciplines. One recommendation from this seminar called for reconciling the demands of the disciplines and the demands of the learners and society by considering the curriculum as consisting of two parts:

One part, to be called the *nuclear* curriculum, would contain materials from the disciplines, selected to fulfill those objectives of education which are determined primarily by the needs of the developing child and the aims imposed by our culture and society. . . .

The second, or *cortical,* component of the curriculum would be chosen by contrary and complementary principles. It would consist of materials chosen specifically because they are representative of the major disciplines.[8]

This recommendation was in answer to an unresolved issue in curriculum organization: Should the schools organize for furthering the acquisition of knowledge in a field or should they organize for the application of knowledge and information to the problems of "the man on the street"? The answer was "both."

Practical ways for organizing nuclear and cortical curricula in schools have yet to be demonstrated. As indicated in Chapter 3, we recommend the teaching of disciplines drawn from the humanities, physical and life science, mathematics, and the social sciences. It is important that the cortical curriculum be seen as emphasizing investigatory procedures and rejecting the pretense of covering the field of knowledge. Reliance is placed instead on apprehension of a system of basic concepts and modes of inquiry.

One should not confuse the cortical-curriculum emphasis on concepts with the older subject-matter curriculum and its emphasis on canned "concepts" or generalizations. In the older organization of such a subject as social studies, for instance, it was common to present summary statements divorced from a system of knowledge and maneuver conclusions that either supported a particular social value (prescriptive knowledge) or those that one would not apply ("Men are interdependent, therefore, we should all like each other." "Different waters of the world present different problems to navigation." Dah!)

Although school systems have been remarkably quick to accept disciplines representative of the physical and life sciences and mathematics, they may be more reluctant to accept those from the social sciences. The idea of permitting children to be objective about social phenomena and to view the human predicament as seen through the analytical eyes of an economist, sociologist, or political scientist would be about as great an educational revolution as has ever appeared. In introducing the social

[8] National Education Association, *The Scholars Look at the Schools,* A Report of the Disciplines Seminar, June 1961. Washington, D.C.: National Education Association, 1962, p. 51.

sciences into curriculum, the administration will find it necessary to reassure his community that traditional loyalties to society's values are very much alive in the nuclear curriculum, even if not found in the cortical.

The outline below represents an effort to give the learners opportunity for sampling major domains of knowledge and for ap-

Excerpted Schedule of Program of Studies

Grade	Cortical	Nuclear
10	1. Literature or Fine Arts 2. Mathematics 3. Biology	4. Specific problems of local import which reflect general social issues, e.g., peace, population, resources and roles of government. ("How shall we zone our community?")
11	1. Sociology, Anthropology, History, Economics 2. Mathematics 3. Chemistry	5. Activity program in correction of individual deficiencies in: a. habits of reading, writing, arithmetic, manners and morals; and physical abilities.
12	1. Philosophy or Religion 2. Mathematics 3. Physics	b. pursuit of special interests, e.g., foreign language, another discipline, or vocational activity.

plying that knowledge in problems of personal and social significance. The nuclear offerings (4,5) are offered each year parallel to the sample of disciplines (cortical offerings) scheduled.

The unit suggested in the outline "How shall we zone our community?" is an illustration of an organizing center reflecting a core curriculum. It could contribute to the development of practical intelligence, accentuating skills of discussion and decision which make for effective living within the society, and, perhaps, a personal commitment and action in accordance with the previous development in this experience. A problem such as zoning requires the application of principles and outlooks found in the fields of aesthetics, sociology, economics, political science, and the like.

The application of theories of principles and basic concepts learned in the disciplines is, of course, one way of strengthening a weakness in cortical organization, namely, failure to meet the criteria of integration. In the latter center of organization, organizational elements and instructional objectives are largely predetermined by the national committees of scholars and educators who prepare the materials.

In the nuclear curriculum local leaders can select those social problems which are of great local importance and of concern to particular students as organizing centers for the courses and units. A word of caution: The problems selected should be those which will give rise to organizing elements of universal value. This will not be difficult, because most local problems of interest are instances of larger issues facing humanity.

The nuclear curriculum in its activity program requires that teachers select organizing centers which are most in accord with the personal educative desires (not mere whims which lead to blind alleys) and the demands made by society upon particular learners. The scheduling of these offerings need not be uniform in frequency and duration. Class periods in which the application of knowledge is paramount should be for several hours at a time, but need only be scheduled two or three times each week. Class periods concerned with the development of abstractions necessary to the disciplines can be scheduled for 30 or 45 minutes. However, these periods should be scheduled more frequently.

Breadth versus Depth in Curriculum Organization

Ideally, each offering in the cortical program will continue once it is introduced. That is, if literature as a systematic study is taken by a pupil in the 10th grade, he should continue with literature as a discipline in the 11th and 12th grades. This may not be possible for at least two reasons: (a) he must sample other disciplines, and (b) instructional materials for teaching the discipline in cortical fashion over several-year periods are not available.

The newer curriculum materials in the disciplines are usually year-long courses of study (like PSSC) or units within a field (like "The Meaning of Civilization," a unit which introduces learners to anthropology as a discipline).

A true curriculum (a series of related offerings K–12) featuring a disciplinary approach developed by national study groups is presently found only in mathematics. It is expected that other fields will eventually have organized programs for continuous instruction over several years.

The activity program will permit many youngsters to continue a study in one of the disciplines while sampling others in the prescribed cortical program. This means, however, that a discipline taught only for a short time, say as a semester or year-long course of study, must be educative if not complete. One need not always pursue a study under formal direction for several years in order to get a payoff in learning. A brief exploration in the discipline might focus on how to study the field independently.

Schools must stop increasing the number and diversity of courses they offer each year. Excessive curricular expansion produces a poorer, rather than a better, education. Sometimes more frugal policies have more educative consequences than expensive ones. Basic instruction in a field is more appropriate than many courses dealing with specialized treatments of the field. One of Joel Hildebrand's contributions to educational thought is applicable here. The Hildebrand Law states that the number of courses offered by a college department (school) is inversely proportional to the intellectual distinctions of its faculty and the amount of basic knowledge in the field.

A recently concluded study on "The Effect of a Depth versus a Breadth Method of Art Instruction at the Ninth Grade Level"[9] showed the importance of depth in an activity rather than a survey of activities in a field. A depth program was defined as one which allows sustained concentration in one area of study. There was variety within the area, but the different activities were linked by organizing elements for sequential and cumulative elements. A breadth program was one in which a variety of well-chosen topics and activities were dispersed to accomodate differences in the interests and experiences of pupils. A survey type of introduction to many media was an example of breadth. The study showed that the depth method produced the greater gain in individual student progress in the arts over a one-year period. Students preferred the breadth approach but learned less from it. One conclusion was that sustained work in a limited area of activity (e.g., painting) is a better way to develop a positive, aesthetic, self-determining orientation to the arts. It allows a step-by-step method, with objectives clearly delineated, as opposed to a holistic method in which procedures are not analyzed and the learner has difficulty in abstracting the key ideas and methods in the field because of the variety of activities presented in such a short time span.

Organization for Acquisition of Concepts versus Organization for Application of Concepts

Confusion exists over the method of arranging many concrete instances in order to formulate essential skills and abstractions, as opposed to the presentation of an enriched environment for the purpose of applying abstractions already formulated in a complex setting.

Classroom organization in the elementary school is chiefly for the purpose of arranging a sufficient number of concrete activities from which a central idea will be abstracted. The harbor or

[9] Edward L. Mattil, Robert C. Burkhart, Kenneth R. Beittel, and Herbert J. Burgart, "The Effect of a 'Depth' vs. a 'Breadth' Method of Art Instruction at the Ninth Grade Level," *Studies in Art Education,* Vol. 3, No. 1, Fall 1961.

airport unit, for instance, might serve to formulate the economic concept "specialization." But if the teacher makes the harbor unit rich in detail, the learner may never see that which is necessary for formulating the concept. Also, the harbor unit should be undertaken only with the idea of formulating a few abstractions, not to teach all concepts which are present in the situation.

In short, there is a difference between arranging a concrete environment for concept formation and arranging a concrete environment for the application of concepts. The former can be quite simple, even to the point of being sterile; the other, calling for application, can be "life-like" in its complexity. Concept formation calls for organizing principles of sequence; concept application calls for organizing principles of integration.

Additional Readings

Association for Supervision and Curriculum Development, 1958 Yearbook, *A Look at Continuity in the School Program*. Washington, D.C.: National Education Association, 1958.

Beauchamp, George A., *Curriculum Theory*. Wilmette, Illinois: Kagg Press, 1961.

Goodlad, John I., *Planning and Organizing for Teaching*. Washington, D.C.: National Education Association, 1963.

Herrick, Virgil E., "The Concept of Curriculum Design," in *Toward Improved Curriculum Theory*. Chicago: University of Chicago Press, 1950, pp. 37–51.

Mackenzie, Gordon N., "What Should be the Organizing Elements of the Curriculum?" in *Toward Improved Curriculum Theory*. Chicago: University of Chicago Press, 1950, pp. 51–59.

Smith, B. Othanel, William O. Stanley, and J. Harlan Shores, "Patterns of Curriculum Organization," Part Three of *Fundamentals of Curriculum Development*. New York: Harcourt, Brace, World, Inc., 1957, pp. 229–425.

Tyler, Ralph W., "The Organization of Learning Experiences," in *Toward Improved Curriculum Theory*. Chicago: University of Chicago Press, 1950, pp. 59–68.

VI. Selecting Materials, Activities, and Teaching Methods

BEFORE ADOPTING TEXTBOOKS, selecting laboratory equipment, hiring teachers, or administering achievement tests, leaders of school systems should be clear about the changes they are trying to effect in learners. They must first be able to indicate the observable differences instruction is to make in the behavior of the learners at hand. Then they can select the stimuli (e.g., books, films, teachers) and arrange the conditions (e.g., lectures, discussions, size of classes) that will produce these changes. In the past, instructional materials and activities have been selected on the basis of an *internal validity,* that is, the instruments and conduct of instruction were judged on the criterion of attractiveness (e.g., textbook selection on the basis of format, use of color, size of print, and price) or whether or not they represented traditional content or practice that the judges had themselves experienced and valued. Evidence was seldom collected to show the *external validity* of the artifacts, that is, it was not demonstrated that the instruments and practices contributed to the effecting of desired behavioral changes.

A suggested way for moving schools toward the better procedure of external validation is planned deletion and substitution of existing practices and tools and the noting of consequences. If removal of certain materials and methods makes no observable differences in the developing of abilities in learners, then what difference do they make?

There are guidelines for the selection of instructional stimuli

91

(e.g., materials, methods, learning opportunities). The use of these guidelines, founded on psychological principles and educational experience, promises more success in changing human behavior than chance selections. Nevertheless, the "art" of teaching, unidentified variables which operate in the actual teaching act, and the personality of the teacher confound the science of curriculum, the planning of instruction in accordance with rational choices. We hold that the guidelines for selection and arrangement of conditions for effective teaching are not recipes which will guarantee success in all school systems. Teaching will remain an art for a long time. Probably 95 per cent of school gain is the result of indescribable factors in the art of teaching. If through the application of principles of curriculum we increase efficiency (achievement, change in behavior) by 5 per cent, it will be an important gain. Businesses go bankrupt on a loss of 5 per cent or less.

Two assumptions are basic to discussion of materials and activities. The first assumption is that any activity or material can be used to further a variety of purposes. Subject matter does not lie in the object and event, but in the thought processes and methods stimulated by these artifacts. If one is shown a chair and asked "What is its subject matter?" he could answer the chair can be physics, history, or art, depending upon the question it generates and the aspects to which one attends when viewing the chair. This is not to say that all materials and events are equally appropriate in the stimulation of desired reactions. Some are far more rich in that they give rise to more interpretations and responses of a particular kind. A copy of Julius Caesar can be used to develop (a) political generalizations about current governmental organization; (b) questions about the validity of astrology and the nature of science; (c) familiarity with an increasing number of authors who have made significant contributions to our culture; (d) ability to go beyond the written word to implications; (e) an unlimited number of other objectives. Experience is not found in the material itself; it is a product of the interaction between the learner and the material. The mental responses, attitudes, and methods of political science, physical science, literature, and many other disciplines can be brought to bear and can be developed from a single concrete event or work of art, depending upon the intellectual thought process of the teacher and the learner.

To the extent that the teacher knows the thought processes, e.g., questions and responses, of his subject matter and is able to recognize their relevancy to new situations (that is, in forms different from those in which they were acquired), he can utilize an unlimited number of materials and activities in helping the learner acquire the intellectual development sought. If the teacher himself does not know the function of his subject matter (the mental responses, attitudes, and methods of the field) and cannot recognize their presence in new forms, then he will never be able to select learning opportunities, to arrange conditions that will elicit the desired behavior. Even if a child showed examples of the desired mental activity, this teacher would be unable to encourage the behavior because he would not recognize it.

When we say that teaching is a creative activity, we mean that there are an inexhaustable number of resources and arrangements of materials to further desired behavior. This can be demonstrated by specifying a new objective before a group of teachers and asking them how they would develop the behavioral change and what materials they would use. No two teachers will present identical solutions to the problem. They will differ in their choices of kinds and amounts of materials, in ordering the steps of presentation, and in the kinds of participation they would demand from learners.

The second assumption regarding responsibility for decisions about selection of materials and activities is that such responsibility must be given only to those who have the intellectual ability in the field of knowledge at hand and the practical intelligence for making judgments consistent with the role of the school.

As we have said, not all teachers are able to prepare effective plans for instruction, and their central weakness is inability to recognize the function of subject matter in new situations. Because teachers differ in this ability, it has been necessary to remove the intellectual responsibility for curriculum development from some teachers and place it in the hands of those who prepare textbooks and teaching materials. Programed instruction is the latest of teaching materials designed to overcome the limitations brought by poorly prepared teachers. Workbooks, teachers' manuals, annotated textbooks with supplementary lists of suggested activities are other ways to compensate for the absence of qualified teachers. One further illustration is the newly produced series of educational records of classics for teachers of literature. Records with the titles "A Man for All Seasons," "The School for Scandal," "Lord of the Flies," and "Macbeth" are available. With each record, a booklet containing the exact text, a series of talks about the work and the author's technique, and a set of "notes for teachers" are provided.

An indication of the kinds of curriculum responsibilities which can be given teachers in relation to their range of ability to select materials and activities can be seen in the diagram on opposite page.

The teacher in Level III cannot be entrusted to select the concept to be taught and must follow the text and workbook; the teacher in Level II might be able to select from among a number of concepts present in a course of study; the teacher in Level I is able to select the pertinent abstractions from his knowledge in the field. Likewise, the teacher in Level III is to be given only limited responsibility for selecting activities, facts, and materials; the textbook carries major direction. The teacher in Level II is allowed to permit children to contribute to the development of the curriculum but must still rely heavily on the decisions made by textbook publishers. Teachers in Level I can select with pupils from among the many cultural resources of the community.

The amount of time to be spent on activities and subject matter is (a) a cooperative decision by teachers in Level I, their pupils, and the school as a whole; (b) a matter for Level II teachers and the school to decide; and (c) a responsibility largely decided by the arrangements of the textbooks used and school directives when Level III teachers are involved.

Decisions about evaluation and next steps to be taken also depend upon the level of the teacher. At Level III, the teacher's evaluations are in terms of the facts covered by the text, not in terms of the application of concepts to other important ideas and particular situations. At Level I, the teacher is engrossed in such questions as appear following the diagram on opposite page.

Levels of Teacher Responsibility in Planning Instructional Programs*

(Read in this direction ──────→)

Areas of Planning	Level III determined by	Level II determined by	Level I determined by
Concept to be taught	Text or workbook	Text and course of study	Design of curriculum in subject field.
Experiences, facts, activities, materials	Text, workbook, and teacher	Text, teacher, group of children	Teacher, group of children, and resources of community in which they live
Timing and time schedules	Text, workbook, teachers, and school program	Teacher and school program	Teacher, group of children, school program
Evaluations	Text, workbook, teacher, school evaluation program	Teacher, concept to be learned, evaluation program	Children, teachers, and school evaluation
Continuities and next steps	Text, workbook, and articulation of school program	Text, course of study, teacher	Design of curriculum, teacher, group of children

* Adapted from: Virgil E. Herrick, "The Concept of Curriculum Design," in Virgil E. Herrick and Ralph W. Tyler, eds., *Toward Improved Curriculum Theory.* Supplementary Educational Monograph No. 71. Chicago: University of Chicago Press, 1950. Copyright © 1950 by The University of Chicago.

What questions or problems do these children have which may serve as vehicles for developing this concept and showing its relationships to other important concepts?

What kind of learning experiences, materials, and processes are important in dealing with this concept?

How rapidly should we move and to what degree can these children understand this concept at this time?

Are they gaining in competency to think, apply, generalize, and see relationships?

How can we lay the foundations for developing our next concept or a more adequate understanding of the old?[1]

Guidelines for Selection of Materials and Activities

1. There must be opportunity for the learner to practice the mental responses, actions, or whatever behavioral changes are intended. Therefore, before deciding to offer a field trip, a film, or a particular book to pupils, one must ask: "Is this material or activity most likely to give rise to the behavior I want?" A simple case will illustrate this. A certain school system had an objective which called for learners to take responsibility as citizens, including the recognition of people's differences and conflicting interests. However, examination of titles not accepted in the school library and activities not allowed in classes revealed that anything that was controversial or contained an element of risk, e.g., activities in which pupils might not use wisely the limited power given them in an activity of consequence, had been eliminated. This kind of inconsistency between ends and means is most miseducative.

In choosing among three textbooks in mathematics treating the multiplication of two rational numbers, it is noted that one uses expressions such as "inverting the divisor," "dropping the denominator"; another is more precise by using words like "addend," "subtrahend," "mixed number"; and the third uses the most precise language of mathematicians, "variables," "symbols for relations, qualifiers" and such symbols as $\forall$ a, b $\neq$, o, c_1, d $\neq$ o, $\frac{a}{b} \times \frac{c}{d} = \frac{ac^1}{bd^1}$. If the objectives call for the development of ability to state the mathematical generalizations precisely, the last text would be preferred on the single criterion of opportunity to practice. However, additional guidelines must be considered before the selection is made.

[1] Virgil E. Herrick, "The Concept of Curriculum Design," in *Toward Improved Curriculum Theory*, Supplementary Educational Monograph No. 71. Chicago: The University of Chicago Press, 1950, p. 49. Copyright © 1950 by The University of Chicago Press.

2. The learning opportunity (stimulus, material, activity, teacher) must be within the comprehension of the learners. At the classroom level it would be ridiculous to give a child a book to read and expect him to respond to the printed words if he could neither attack unfamiliar printed words or recall the particular words sighted in the book. However, the violation of this principle at the administrative level is a frequent occurrence. For instance, we are currently hearing about school systems which are offering programs for "the culturally deprived youth." These programs are intended to raise the level of expectations and horizons of learners from low socioeconomic homes or substrata culture. The answer to the problem of changing tastes and raising expectations will not occur merely by exposing these learners to the great exemplars of our culture in museums, concerts, and the theater. These learners must first acquire the ability to participate in the opportunities. Before selecting an art exhibit for learners, there should be assurance that pupils know how to greet works of art, e.g., how to use balance, feeling of space, color, nonrepresentational content, and the degree of subjectivity allowed the viewer. Similarly, it is miseducative to place pupils with a teacher who is not able to communicate at the level of the intended learner.

3. The stimulus should be consistent with the "likes," not the "dislikes," of the learners. If pupils have learned to avoid materials which are heavily weighted with printed verbalism, i.e., have found the materials unrewarding, then such materials should not be selected for immediate use. Intervening materials which feature more concrete illustrations and gradually prepare learners to handle the verbalism at a later date would be more appropriate.

This guideline can be used by a principal in assigning teachers to particular groups of pupils. A teacher can be categorized as an instrument of instruction just as much as a textbook or film, and, therefore, is subject to the same principles for selection. For instance, Ruth Landis has said that Mexican-American children are accustomed to authoritarian procedures with the personal touch. The teacher for these children must be one who exercises leadership in a continuous fashion, even to the point of nagging. The Mexican-American learner is, however, reassured by a show of emotion on the part of the teacher and sees the typical American teacher's attempt to be objective as "cold" and "punitive."[2] Therefore, in selecting teachers for these pupils, the school might attain instructional objectives more readily by assigning to them a teacher who is capable of establishing intense personal relations rather than one who acts in accordance with the more customary "Anglo" value of "objectivity."

The central point here is that before making a selection one must find out for what the prospective learners have been rewarded in the past. Studies of learners in general will not enable one to make an accurate prediction. The administrator of the school must find out what has been rewarding for the range of pupils for whom he is responsible, and the teacher must get similar information for the particular members of his class. Learning opportunities must be adapted at both administrative and classroom levels accordingly.

4. The learning contact should contribute to several instructional objectives. This criterion is stated with some reservation. Sometimes we say that it is better to teach one thing at a time— a partial truth. The formulation of powerful ideas may often best occur in simple situations rather than from complex stimuli. However, a complementary principle is that a complex stimulus may contribute to the development of more ideas than a simple one. The lasting popularity of classics like *Julius Caesar* is due to the fact that they lend themselves to a range of interpretations. When we have several objectives to reach in a limited time, it is desirable to select the learning opportunity which will advance the learner simultaneously toward several objectives, provided it will not cause interference in the acquisition of a crucial understanding. The choosing of a contact which contributes to several objectives instead of the contact which advances only one is sometimes called the principle of economy. An illustration can be found in the Soviet practice of teaching the concept of percentage from content revealing the ratio of Negroes and whites to total unemployed in the United States.

[2] Ruth Landis, "Cultural Factors in Counselling," *The Journal of General Education,* Vol. XV, No. 1, April 1963, pp. 55–67.

Basic Forms for Administering Instruction

A visit to any school will reveal pupils engaged in one or more typical learning situations. Professor Erick Lindman has suggested that these situations can be typed as: independent study, group discussion, lecture, supervised laboratory practice or project, and tutoring. The mark of a good administrator is the extent to which these forms are appropriately used. By "appropriately" we mean the matching of a basic form to the kind of instructional objective sought. If, for instance, the school is expecting all youngsters merely to *acquire* information on a given topic (ability to state and recall), it would be more appropriate to bring all the learners together for instruction by lecture or other mass media (television, radio, common readings) than to use a situation calling for group discussion. Although the latter is desirable for attaining objectives involving human interaction, it does not compare favorably with the lecture in terms of the amount of information which can be transmitted in a short time.

If, on the other hand, a school wants learners to reach an objective calling for knowledge of methodology in a subject and problem-solving ability as well as factual recall of information, it would be more economical to place learners in a situation calling for laboratory practice or projects in which acquisition of facts would occur along with the methods of inquiry.

Team teaching is an example of an innovation that permits a variety of learning situations economically in terms of the task at hand. Under team teaching, the advantages of the lecture with a faster rate of transmission of information can be given to many, while the advantages of interpersonal exchanges are available in small groups. Ordinarily, it does not matter in the least whether pupils see a film in a group of 5 or 200. Conversely, the diagnosis and remedial steps of a peculiar error being made in composition by an individual may best occur in a tutoring situation between the learner and the teacher.

When used properly, the language laboratory and teaching machines are especially economical for those objectives which can only be obtained through frequent overt responding and confirmation. By way of example, under traditional administrative organization the foreign language classroom might allow each pupil a total of three hours a year in which to orally respond in the foreign language and to have his response confirmed. (e.g., 45 minutes daily instruction and 45 pupils allow each child only 1 minute for oral responding during the class session if the opportunity is equally distributed.) Obviously, this is an inadequate amount of time for development of verbal fluency. With a properly programed teaching machine or language laboratory, the child has as many opportunities to respond in one day's period as he has in a year under a traditional arrangement.

Matching Learning Situations to Educational Objectives

In the compendium *Taxonomy of Educational Objectives*[3] cognitive processes are ordered into six areas of complexity: (1) *recall* of knowledge (information); (2) the simple level of *comprehension* in which one understands without seeing the full implications of the matter dealt with; (3) *application* of abstractions such as general ideas and principles to concrete situations; (4) *analysis* of material into constituent parts to clarify it; (5) *synthesis* of the elements so as to form a whole or pattern not previously existing; and (6) *evaluation,* judging the value of materials and methods, the establishing of standards and the exercising of judgment in their application.

The diagram below contains a problem for the reader. His task is to match teaching situations with cognitive processes sought in learners. For instance, if one believes that lecture is the most economical way to help learners acquire and recall information, he will put an *x* in the square opposite *lecture* and under the heading *recall of information.* Engagement in this problem might correct the present tendency to accept large-group instruction without clear notions as to why it is effective or ineffective for some purposes. Also, after engaging in this task, one will look at a school organization in terms of the efficiency of its learning situations. For instance, the principal of a school would be expected

[3] B. S. Bloom, *Taxonomy of Educational Objectives.* New York: Longmans, Green, 1956.

to be more sensitive to waste in instructional time when several teachers show the same film or use other mass media in separate sessions rather than a common one, although their instructional purposes for learners in the sessions are the same.

	Cognitive Processes					
Learning Situations	*Recall of informa- tion*	*Simple compre- hension*	*Appli- cation*	*Analy- sis*	*Syn- thesis*	*Evalu- ation*
Independent study						
Group dis- cussion and decision						
Lecture						
Tutoring (private conferences)						
Supervised practice and projects						

Answers to the problems should reflect the following considerations:

1. Independent study should be used whenever learners are capable of learning and practicing the task without surveillance. Correspondence courses, programed learning, readings, and other pertinent instructional resources must be available if independent study is to be successful. The key to independent study is in specifying to the learner exactly what he will be asked to demonstrate following the study. Unless he sees the objective and comprehends the level of mastery demanded of him, he will not be able to select relevant data from the resources available.

Further, pupils should be helped to assume initiative and responsibility for self-instruction or independent study by being taught how to apply principles in correcting and improving their own work. For instance, children in elementary school can be taught to discover and correct their own errors. The ideal of helping the pupil learn how to formulate problems, find answers, and evaluate himself is gaining in popularity. Independent study programs often accompany such a goal. Usually only pupils who have high ability and background in the area undertake independent study because others might be overwhelmed by the difficulties. The execution of a project is one way of carrying out independent study. The project method is not valued so much for effectiveness in helping learners acquire facts as it is for developing student ability to be resourceful. Incidentally, national merit scholars reported that the requirement of a term paper or laboratory project was one characteristic of their most stimulating course.

As we have said, the success of independent study rests on the learner's being clear as to the expectations held for him at the conclusion of the study and the availability of the resources by which he can organize his own learning experiences to attain these expectations. If a pupil knows he is going to be tested on a factual content of a particular book, it is more advantageous for him to read that book independently than to participate in the classroom with its lectures, recitations, and various other activities. Discussions and lectures apparently interfere with learning the textbook and its particular plan of organization.

Independent study need not point toward examinations based on textbooks. Suppose a school wanted to further "creative thought." We believe that in order for this kind of thinking to occur, one must have possession of such factors as sensitivity to problems, fluency in ideas, and ability to synthesize, analyze and evaluate. Therefore, the school could arrange conditions to promote these factors.

Some of these conditions can best be met through independent study. Patrick's summary[4] of the conditions favorable for develop-

---

[4] Catherine Patrick, "Creative Thinking," *Encyclopedia of Psychology,* Philip L. Harriman, ed. New York: The Philosophical Library, Inc., 1946, pp. 110–13.

ing creative thought include: (1) time not too strictly limited, (2) the problem sufficiently difficult, (3) frequent relaxation and change of activities from those representing the central problem, (4) periods of idleness in which autistic thinking may promote imaginative ideas, (5) spirit of optimism, (6) relaxing pressure of ordered routine to allow more free time, and (7) close imitative study of good models. Very few of the foregoing conditions now prevail in schools. If we prize creativity, then we should experiment in making these conditions available to pupils in independent study. A far cry from pressuring the child with homework and filling his time out of school with assignments and activities!

2. Group discussion and decision are especially important whenever values (prescriptive knowledge) are to be acted upon. Discussion is not adequate in itself but requires decision. The ability and willingness to apply a principle in new situations will occur only for those groups which have a decision to apply the principle. Discussion without decision is not likely to lead to changed behavior.

Discussion and decision should be used when the category of task is evaluation and involves the making of decisions, the making of policy, and the reconstruction of conduct. Decisions are often judgments made about specific questions of behavior, e.g., "Should I go to college or not?" "Should I smoke?" "Should we abolish capital punishment?" They do, however, commit one to undertake a course of action. Policymaking consists of establishing rules which give consistency from one decision to another, e.g., "What position should I, as a Republican or Democrat, take on the issue of Federal aid to education?" The solution to issues like this rests on a policy associated with the political tenets of the party. Behind decisions and policies are standards and ideals. A change or reconstruction of these standards and ideals is the most fundamental kind of judgment that can occur. Such reconstruction requires a situation which is unresolved and requires decision. It also requires that the individual be personally involved, not just to the extent of wanting an answer, but to the point that he decides to do something in practice about the issue under consideration. Usually schools do not assume responsibility for high-level cognitive processes like evaluation. Typically, instruction is characterized by (a) the finding of facts about a situation and (b) contemplating and reflecting upon these facts, and (c) perhaps, an expression of preference and the weighing of values about the situation. The last step occurs infrequently; the step which seldom gets taken at all is committing oneself and acting in accordance with the judgment.

One of the most remarkable set of instructional materials that calls for commitment to premises of this nation and requires acting upon these premises is that produced by the Citizenship Education Project of Teachers College, Columbia University. The effectiveness of these materials has been demonstrated in school systems across the country. We predict a renaissance in the use of these materials as the demand grows for a restoration of balance between the acquisition of descriptive knowledge (science) and prescriptive knowledge (values). In addition to aiding learners in acquiring values, the CEP materials will help these learners to apply values in daily situations outside the school.

Evidence of an effective way to develop knowledge of a field, scientific thinking, intellectual orientation, and resourcefulness in problem-solving is available in reports of the Pyramid Plan.[5] Essentially, this plan is a modification of the discussion form. Each "pyramid group" of students consisted of six freshmen, six sophomores, two juniors who were assistant leaders, and a senior who was the group leader. The pyramid groups met weekly for two-hour periods to discuss personal–vocational goals, requirements for entrance, skills needed for academic success, the significance of their courses for their goals, issues, and the central concepts of the discipline. The group leaders worked with a faculty member in defining objectives, discussing small-group techniques, and defining issues to be considered by the pyramid groups. The results were most positive, far exceeding attainment of objectives by students who received a special program of lectures, films, and demonstrations.

[5] C. R. Carpenter, "The Penn State Pyramid Plan: Interdependent Student Work Study Groupings for Increasing Motivation for Academic Development," paper read at the 14th National Conference on Higher Education, Chicago, March 1959.

In relating the form of learning situations to the task of developing cognitive processes, we are struck with an inconsistency in the ordering of instructional forms as found in schools. Lectures are best for the acquisition of information; discussions and projects are best for the development of problem-solving skills. Since problem-solving ordinarily requires information, we should expect discussion to be more effective with learners who have information than for those who lack background. Incidentally, at least one empirical study supports this hypothesis. Melton, Feldman, and Mason[6] found that lectures were more effective than discussion for children in Grades 5, 6, and 7, but discussions were more effective for eighth-graders. Yet, large lecture sessions are found more frequently at advanced levels where learners have better backgrounds, and discussion groups are more common at the secondary and elementary levels of schooling. In the future, we may see increased reliance upon lectures in elementary schools when the lectures are given in concrete terms, as opposed to verbalism which does not allow the teacher to communicate with young learners.

3. Tutoring or holding individual conferences, with its emphasis upon decision, is likely to be especially necessary for the learning of higher cognitive processes. Variability among learners increases with the difficulty of the task. For instance, in a simple task of learning to spell there is little need for tutoring; the range of peculiar questions raised by learners is narrow. In a complex task like comprehension and analysis in reading there is need for "branching" or attending to individual differences. Consequently, the cost of instructional time mounts when a school undertakes the development of intelligence. A school that is content with factual recall and simple comprehension can operate on an austerity budget. In fact, correspondence courses and televised instruction will produce as high scores on achievement tests of recall and comprehension as instruction by classroom teachers.

Parenthetically, an economical curriculum is one in which maximum learning, e.g., achievement of high mental powers, occurs in less time for less money. It is a false economy to spend

[6] A. W. Melton, N. G. Feldman, and C. N. Mason, *Experimental Studies of the Education of Children in a Museum School.* Washington, D.C.: American Association Museums, 1936.

relatively small amounts and not develop the intellectual powers actually demanded. There can be considerable saving by making sure that supervised practice, group discussion (decision), and tutoring are not relegated to information-dispensing. It is a simple matter to hold youngsters accountable for the recall of particular information and then to make the sources of this information available in films, books, and other materials. In this case, no instruction is necessary, only an examination after independent study. Tutoring, so necessary for assisting the individual who has questions and deficiencies peculiar to himself, should not be used for dealing with problems common to the group.

4. In contrasting laboratory instruction with other forms, we find that the laboratory is not so efficient in transmission of information as those forms which present abstractions orally or in print. Films and demonstrations may short-cut some of the trial and error of the laboratory. It is far better to develop the understanding of concepts than to teach students to solve problems by going through a routine series of sensorimotor steps. Laboratory effectiveness in developing understanding and problem-solving skills depends upon the teacher's emphasis on concepts and problem-solving procedures rather than following a manual.

As indicated, in Chapter 1, the laboratory, with its emphasis upon discovery is likely to be effective only when the teacher knows a number of different ways in which the principles to be discovered can be found.

Although the laboratory may not be the most effective means to formulating concepts, it has great promise as a situation for learning how to apply concepts. In the process of laboratory applications, one must be taught how to identify variables which prevent principles or concepts acquired in other settings from operating in the particular instances and what a principle looks like in concrete form. There is considerable evidence that learning to apply principles in the complex environment of "real life" is more difficult than formulating the principles as the result of experiences in formal instruction. To date, most programs in schools have not gone much beyond accepting responsibility for the learner's acquisition of concepts.

Scheduling of Learning Situations

Trump and Baynham have suggested[7] a number of ways in which schedules can be modified so that pupils and teachers can break out of the conventional standard organizational plan and match learning situations to learning tasks. They foresee that the school of the future will schedule students in class groups only 18 hours a week. The average student at the tenth-grade level will spend about 12 of the 18 hours in large-group instruction (lecture) and six in small-group discussion. On the average, 12 hours each week in school will be spent in individual independent study. Thus, most students will continue to spend about 30 hours a week in regular offerings as they do now. But they will find it possible to spend more time because school facilities will be open to them.

The lecture–TV classes (150 or more students) will be scheduled for approximately 40 minutes; group discussion with 15 or fewer pupils will meet for longer periods of time but less frequently; independent study will occur inside and outside of school hours. Time for conferences with individuals can occur as teachers are freed from routine tasks and the uneconomical practice of information-dispensing in small groups by teachers. Students who can profitably spend several hours at one period in a laboratory or in work experiences will find it possible to do so.

One modified schedule is to leave open several periods in the secondary school day. During this time, pupils can attend lectures, discussions, laboratory, and do independent study without conflicting with the less flexible offerings scheduled during other periods of the day. Another plan is to schedule classes for four days a week. One full day a week then can be used for classes of varied sizes, independent study, and other learning activities which do not lend themselves to conventional school periods. The scheduling of various forms of learning situations permits modifying the forms themselves. A lecture can also include a demonstration and discussion. Television can be used for tutorial interaction between teacher and pupil by incorporating principles of programed learn-

[7] J. Lloyd Trump and Dorsey Baynham, *Focus on Change: Guide to Better Schools.* Chicago: Rand McNally & Company, 1961.

ing; programed material demanding continuous response from the learner can be presented by television. Also, imaginative teaching can occur in large lecture halls in which the lecture calls for visual projections, recorded sounds, and ETV presentation. Microphones and response panels throughout the auditorium permit pupils to ask and answer questions.

Learning Opportunities and the Meeting of Individual Differences

There can be no profitable planning in response to the fact of individual differences until one faces the issue: Do I want all learners to acquire the same behavior or do I want all learners to increase in their variability? As we indicated in Chapter 4, schools must do both. Within the nuclear curriculum, some offerings will try to shape behavior to common ends; others will try to increase variability among persons, giving more attention to individual objectives. Core programs, with their social problem-solving situations involving value judgments, advance the cause of common outlooks and develop in everyone a similar character or class of response to social stimuli, although the specific response and level of mastery varies with each individual. Activity programs, on the other hand, are truly planned to permit the individual to pursue his own purposes which are not necessarily held in common with others.

Terms like "individualization of instruction" do not carry shared meanings. Some would only concern themselves with the fact of individual differences because they know that unless these differences are taken into account the school cannot get control over the learner to shape him in the direction *the school wants to see him go*. Others take individual differences into account in order to find out how the school can best help the individual become that which *he wants to become*. Those holding the first position are something like the advertiser who samples public opinion regarding his product or service. He may do this not to change the product or service, but to find out the kind of publicity campaign necessary to modify opinion of the consumer in favorable ways toward the existing product. The school expresses both positions through the core and discipline curriculum (required) and the activity curriculum (elective).

ADAPTATION TO THE INDIVIDUAL LEARNER AT TWO LEVELS IN THE SCHOOL SYSTEM

There are advantages to distinguishing learning opportunities that are selected at the institutional level (school-wide) and opportunities that are best manipulated at the classroom level. The availability of information is not the same at both levels, therefore, decision-making should occur at the point of greatest perspective. At the institutional level, boards of education, superintendents, and directors of instruction wrestle with problems of individualization when they consider graduation requirements, course offerings, and selection and assignment of teachers to classes. These decisions require information from the larger social sphere not readily available to the local teacher. At the classroom level, the qualified teacher assumes major responsibility for decisions relevant to adapting instructional materials and methods to the idiosyncrasies of particular learners present, something very difficult to do from a distance.

Administrators serve individualization best when they establish opportunities that fulfill the functions of integration, specialization, supplementation, and exploration. If any one of these functions is not taken into account, individualization of instruction will be weakened. Among the factors which can be manipulated at the administrative level in individualizing the program of the school are graduation requirements, programs of studies, honors courses, opportunities for advanced placement, and various kinds of teachers. All should be matched with the pupils and instructional objectives in mind. It is important to specify to a newly assigned teacher the functions his classroom is to discharge. The school is less effective, for example, when a teacher of a course designed as specialistic by school officials starts varying objectives in terms of personal interests of pupils instead of holding all pupils to the requirements of the field. Likewise, the advantages of planned instruction disappears when the teacher in a core curriculum attempts to hold all students accountable to the standards and absolute level of performance demanded in a discipline.

Institutional-level decisions regarding courses, materials, and teachers should follow the guidelines given at the beginning of this chapter. The same guidelines also apply for teachers in the operation of their classrooms. Usually, however, the classroom teacher has a different set of specific factors to manipulate. The following are artifacts that the teacher can modify in adapting instruction to individual differences:

1) frequency of praise and special privileges given the individual

2) amount of review

3) degree to which the task is specified for the individual

4) degree of freedom in selecting ways to proceed on the task

5) amount of freedom to select own criteria for evaluating process and product

6) frequency of testing the individual

7) promptness in giving him knowledge of results

8) amount of extra assistance available

9) situations for the learner to work alone, with peers, and with total class; with friends and foes, older and younger persons

10) extent of self-initiated work permitted

11) fluctuation in basis for grade, e.g., effort, absolute achievement, gain

12) amount of time allowed for completion of assignments

13) distractions permitted in room environment, e.g., bulletin boards and color which compete for the teacher's attention are detrimental to the learning of some students.

Additional Readings

A/V Communications Review, Supplement 4, September–October 1961.

Dewey, John, *Experience and Education*. New York: The Macmillan Company, 1938.

Keislar, Evan R., "A Descriptive Approach to Classroom Motivation," *The Journal of Teacher Education*, Vol. XI, No. 2, 310–15.
National Society for the Study of Education, 49th Yearbook, *Learning and Instruction*. Chicago: The University of Chicago Press, 1950.
Symonds, Percival M., *What Education Has to Learn from Psychology*. New York: Teachers College, Columbia University, Bureau of Publications, 1958.

PART IV. EVALUATION

THE TERM *evaluation* has come to mean "I like it" or "I dislike it"—expressions of emotional reaction to programs, activities, processes, whatever one has experienced or is experiencing. A correction is in order. In Chapter 7 procedures for answering the question "How good is our curriculum?" call for objective measurement, not just personal subjective preference. Effort is made to see value judgments as especially important in the selection of the ends sought through instruction, yet an appeal is voiced for more objective assessment of means of instruction. Chapter 7 provides specific direction as to how a school can improve its curriculum by objectively noting the consequences that follow from varying the aspects of curriculum under controlled conditions.

VII. The Quest for Quality

WHEN ENGINEERS design a plan for the construction of a bridge, the essential test of the plan is demonstrated safety of the bridge in terms of its specifications. Other considerations, of course, are the aesthetic and economical features. Business leaders assess their plan of operation chiefly in terms of profit earned following its execution. In medicine, the physician is judged chiefly by his ability to maintain or change the status of health of patients. Too often, however, curriculum plans have not been assessed in terms of consequences, the desirable and undesirable changes brought about in learners. Instead, details within the plan, such as the particular learning experience offered, frequency of schedule, or pattern of classroom organization (e.g., self-contained), have become ends to be sought and defended rather than details to be validated. The consequences of particular curricular arrangements and procedures must be demonstrated; we can no longer afford to be wedded to practices that do not contribute to desirable changes in learners any more than an engineer would be permitted to give his loyalty to a favored design which produced a weakened structure or a physician would be allowed to use a technique known to be harmful.

Many schoolmen oppose the trend to quality control, the collection of evidence regarding the effectiveness of programs. They do this for several reasons. First, they are afraid that evidence will be collected only in respect to recall of information and competency in a few academic skills. In other words, they think that the search for evidence will be limited to the more easily measured aspects of education and will neglect sampling the changes made in higher mental processes and social behavior of learners.

Second, opposers to the use of criterion measures are often process-oriented. They believe that learning occurs under such conditions as warm and friendly pupil teacher interaction, variety of instructional media, and the teacher's awareness of the child's self-concept. Therefore, they make no effort to assess the learning that does occur as a result of these conditions, but only judge whether the conditions are present. They have made the process the end rather than means to be evaluated.

Third, some distrust the way the evidence will be interpreted. They are concerned that those reading the results of school appraisal will not consider factors which have affected this learning and achievement. Some of these factors relate to the nature of the learners, such as variation in their cultural background and teachability (e.g., their level of motivation). They know, too, that it is difficult to pinpoint the causal factors relating to lack of achievement.

Finally, measurement of consequences carries the risk that one may have to revise his assumptions and favored practices, a difficult task for anyone. In making explicit and public the changes desired in learners, one is no longer "free" to impose his own peculiar instructional objectives upon the learner but must be guided by the judgments of a larger social system. Instead of the classroom's being the "teacher's castle," it becomes a unit in an organized system of instruction in which all units contribute to continuity in learning.

Nevertheless, political pressures as well as professional conscience are demanding that more attention be given to collecting evidence regarding the effectiveness of the curriculum. California's new legislative action requiring the reporting of district test results is a case in point. The increasing number of pupils who take the college entrance examinations is another indication of a trend to assessment of consequences of instruction. Project Talent's testing of 450,000 students in secondary schools across the nation and analysis of data collected in these schools in terms of the students' instructional experiences and subsequent successes or failures is also an example of professional interest in improving curriculum.

Evaluation Data Required

The ultimate evaluation of a particular plan for attaining instructional objectives is empirical evidence that the changes in behavior desired of learners has occurred as a result of the plan. However, judgment is still required as to whether a particular plan merits the time, effort, and expense. Evidence regarding the achievement of learners must also be such as to permit an inference regarding the influence of the curriculum itself. An assessment of the curriculum can occur through a post-test given at the end of instruction. But the post-test scores may be due chiefly to other factors. For example, learners may have learned much of what is measured on the post-test from their parents, television, friends, and other informal sources.

Criterion Test

Evaluation of the curriculum can be conducted so that these extraneous factors or incidental influences in learning are controlled. A pre-test can be given to determine the behavior and level of knowledge with which pupils start. This measure serves as a base for determining the amount of gain resulting from the curriculum.

Scores from pre- and post-tests should be reported, indicating the range of scores and the average score for the population of learners. Explicit evidence should be provided of the effectiveness of the program for different kinds of learner characteristics, e.g., mental age, chronological age, socioeconomic level, sex, physical exceptionality.

Tests Must Correspond to Objectives

If the reader will look on page 58, he will note a test design which permits sampling of a number of objectives. It is desirable that performance of pupils be indicated on each of these aspects, e.g., ability to demonstrate qualitative understanding of fundamentals, ability to apply knowledge to unfamiliar situations, ability to draw valid conclusions from observations and data. The system of classification given in the *Taxonomy of Educational Objectives,*[1] ranging from knowledge to evaluation, can be used in ensuring that evidence is collected for all objectives. That is, one first classifies his objectives in categories such as those calling for "low level comprehension," making use of an idea without relating to other ideas, or "high-level synthesis," putting together elements in such a way as to constitute a pattern not clearly there before. Then he proceeds to arrange situations in which learners will provide evidence as to how well they have attained the objectives. All levels of behavior sought, not just low-level behavior, must be sampled.

One of the most important ways an administrator can increase the effectiveness of his school is by contrasting objectives stated by teachers with the actual tests and other informal means of assessment used by teachers. Recognizing discrepancies between grandiose objectives in the area of intellectual development and the simple recall items (who did what?) so frequently used usually leads to improvements and clarification of purpose. If the classification system given in the *Taxonomy* appears too complicated for use by teachers and others, simpler categories of questions and problems can be used to compare objectives with the kinds of evidence that is being collected, e.g., problems and questions which require the learner to:

    a. state—recall
    b. compare—contrast
    c. illustrate—interpret
    d. explain—apply
    e. summarize—evaluate

It is desirable that the performance of pupils be indicated in each category for which there is an objective. This will provide a profile indicating the particular areas of effectiveness as well as weakness, and will be more meaningful than a total score.

[1] Benjamin S. Bloom, ed., *Taxonomy of Educational Objectives.* New York: Longmans, Green and Company, 1956.

Selecting Tests and Other Situations for Collecting Evidence

Excellent descriptions of evaluative instruments and guidelines for their use are found in *Educational Measurement, The Impact and Improvement of School Testing Programs, Mental Measurements Yearbooks* (see Additional Readings list on p. 130), and numerous commercial textbooks on the subject "Evaluating Pupil Progress." All draw attention to the need for selecting situations that really sample behavior the school is seeking to develop and the importance of specifying minimum acceptable performance. Paper-and-pencil tests are only one kind of practical procedure given in these references. Ingenious suggestions are available for observing learners under conditions in which social relations are involved, assessing products made by learners, collecting records of learners' behaviors in and out of school, and noting the learner's predisposition to act in accordance with desirable attitudes and interests. Ways for specifying the criteria of acceptable performance are well discussed in an inexpensive booklet *Preparing Objectives for Programed Instruction* (see p. 130).

More than two appraisals (pre- and post-tests) are recommended, because additional aspects of program effectiveness are *retention* and *savings*. A follow-up study of graduates is an example of an effort to collect evidence that knowledge is retained (*retention*). *Savings* is the economy realized in learning something faster on a second trial after one has forgotten much of the initial learning. It is strange, but only occasionally do school people collect evidence to show that persons who have undergone instruction in an area can relearn the material or similar material in less time than other persons (savings), although this ability is indeed a valuable one.

Standardized tests of achievement are not always appropriate to a particular instructional program, even when they are described in similar language. Tests must be examined to be sure that they contain items relevant to the terminal behaviors sought by the school. It is to be expected that schools will modify standardized instruments by dropping out irrelevant material and questions which are not appropriate for certain learners. This is seldom done, however. Educators often are reluctant to modify a published instrument, although it is desirable for them to do so. Only when test results are not being collected for the benefit of particular learners but for state-wide and national comparisons is test modification questionable. Whenever the particular learners and local objectives are of primary importance, modifications are in order.

Standardized tests selected to measure attainment of regional and national objectives should be balanced with locally prepared tests which provide evidence regarding the attainment of local and individual objectives. Locally developed instruments are especially necessary in assessing objectives consistent with the school's supplementary functions. Results from both standardized and locally prepared tests can, of course, facilitate discovery of strengths and weaknesses in learning and suggest new instructional objectives.

New Courses of Study Require New Tests

Before one uses any test for purposes of evaluation, it must be compared with the objectives and content of the course of instruction. Recently, we have seen a number of studies to determine whether students in newer mathematics courses do as well as students in conventional courses on traditional mathematics achievement tests. The results suggest that students exposed to the new courses do as well on tests designed for the older curriculum and score higher on tests designed specifically to measure achievement in the newer mathematics.[2] It would not be surprising, however, if those completing newer programs did less well on tests designed for traditional offerings which have different objectives. The intent of the newer courses is to produce behaviors in learners different from those produced by older courses. An illustration of acting responsibly in this matter of matching courses to tests is seen in the practice by the College Entrance Examination Board of granting alternative tests to students, depending

[2] Roland R. Payette, "Educational Testing Service Summary Report of the School Mathematics Study Group Curriculum Evaluation." Reports on Student Achievement in SMSG Courses. Newsletter No. 10. Stanford, California: School Mathematics Study Group, 1961, pp. 5–11.

upon the kind of courses taken in different fields and in the same field. One CEEB physics test, for instance, is available and appropriate for students who have taken the newer Physical Science Study Committee course and another CEEB test is offered to students who have completed traditional physics courses. The unique PSSC objectives emphasized basic science rather than applied science and put more emphasis on the laboratory than on number of topics to be covered. The unique traditional objectives emphasized consumer knowledge, the scientific method and application of physics to technology. We would not expect students from the different courses to do equally well on the same test.

Latent Uses of Testing Interference with Improvement of the Curriculum

If a school system selects tests that are known to have low levels of absolute mastery, the results can be publicized to show that the school system is excelling. This desire to report test results which deceptively make the district "look good" is a latent use of tests.

Some popular tests purporting to measure reading vocabulary, comprehension, mechanics of English, spelling, arithmetic, reasoning, and arithmetic fundamentals at a factual level are associated with an unusual number of high scores. On the other hand, few pupils approach mastery on tests developed to measure ability to apply learning from many fields, rather than simply recalling it. A compensating factor for those who would use the more differentiating test is that the results can be reported in terms of pupil gain rather than in absolute mastery. The easier test does not permit those who were at the top of the test at the beginning of the year to show much growth in the subject matter, whether it occurs or not. The test which permits a range of scores and relatively little absolute achievement is more sensitive to changes that occur among all learners during the instructional period. Unless a sensitive test is used, one does not really know whether his instruction is effective or not.

It is very difficult to show that the curriculum plan is indeed making a difference in the lives of learners unless the instrument used in assessing effects is both directly related to the content of the plan and is sensitive enough to measure the effects. Many reports of "no difference" really do not mean that the curriculum has produced no change. They really say "Our tests are not powerful enough to reveal the changes that have occurred."

Analysis of Sub-Parts of a Test is Better than Viewing a Test as a Whole

A total score based on, say, reading, seldom gives enough precise information for focusing upon needed improvement in the curriculum. The test results must be analyzed in terms of sub-objectives within the reading program. One might ask, for instance, "Have learners improved as well in their ability to use context clues as they have in their ability to pronounce initial and final consonants in unfamiliar post-test words?" When specific strengths and weaknesses are identified, there is a better chance of finding cause-and-effect relationships in the curriculum. After finding specific weaknesses, for instance, the teacher can examine the opportunities that were used in teaching for that objective and speculate about their adequacy. Did they fail to meet criteria for selection? Were they not continued long enough? Were interfering stimuli presented at the same time? Were they presented in the proper order? These and other questions can be directed at the identifiable factors which were used in the teaching of the sub-objective. It is more difficult to speculate about all the activities that occurred in teaching of the subject represented in the total test. One should not try to improve performance in reading by modifying all learning opportunities, if the major weakness is inability to perform on a sub-part. For example, don't throw out the "whole-word-sight" reading program to improve a weakness in phonics; rather, introduce "phonics" as an adjunct to the program.

Teaching to the Test

Ideally, objectives and examinations are consistent. One is naïve if he assumes that tests are not instruments for influencing what is taught and judging how well the school is doing its job. Similarly, what most pupils learn in a class is less likely to be influenced by the stated objectives than by those things they are held for on examinations. The notion that it is bad to teach to a test is prevalent. Like so many half-truths in education, this one is miseducative. One should teach to a test when a test represents the objectives, the changes sought through instruction. It is ridiculous to try to improve the learner's marksmanship by blindfolding him and hiding the target. Objections to teaching to tests are valid only when the tests do not reflect the instructional objectives. Some persons are concerned that teachers will present specific answers to test problems and situations so that pupils parrot the answers without understanding the process by which the answer was developed and without knowing why the answer is appropriate. This fear that the pupil will get a high score for the wrong reasons can easily be avoided by making sure that the problem situation is an instance of a class of problems but not identical to the example used in the instructional period. Of course, there are times when just getting the learner to respond correctly to the same situation is a valid objective.

Generally speaking, we try to equip learners to act appropriately in the presence of certain stimuli. "Appropriately" means making a particular response or a class of responses which meet the standards set for behavior in the presence of the stimuli at hand. The pupil must learn the conditions under which these responses are not appropriate, when the stimuli are different in some essential form. Criticism of teaching to tests is usually directed at paired-associate learning, where there is a single response to a single stimulus. Rather than criticizing teaching to tests, it is better to provide tests which permit a range of responses to a range of stimuli. The degree of a learner's understanding can be measured by the number of appropriate responses to a range of stimuli. Rote learning is seen as a correct response to a single stimulus; learning with understanding has been defined as a correct response or responses to a particular situation never seen before but recognized by the learner as a situation within a class of situations to which he has learned how to respond. Before one can demonstrate understanding, he must learn to identify cues or aspects in the problem which make it an instance of the class to which his repertoire of knowledge and action apply.

The use of both standardized tests in class and assessment measures of the learner's behavior in out-of-class settings will help to clarify whether or not objectives calling for development of mental processes are indeed being met. If one distrusts the test, he should get evidence of the learner's ability to use the mental process in other situations. For example, one might want to know how well arithmetic reasoning scores obtained from a standardized test correspond to the learner's ability to solve the same kind of problem in everyday life. If 70 per cent of the learners answer printed problems on interest correctly, say, what per cent of these same pupils can figure out the cost of purchasing their own car on borrowed money?

Improving the Curriculum through Experimentation and Measurement

There are so many factors in a curriculum plan which can influence changes in the learner that it is difficult to know which factors or combinations of factors are relevant. Perhaps the organizing centers are the key to success. Or it might be that the kinds of learning opportunities presented make the difference. Or, perhaps, it is the order in which the learning opportunities occur that is all important. Most likely, major changes in the learner are not so much a product of the curriculum plan as they are of less tangible factors such as "school climate," "teacher personality," and "family situations." Researchers on Project Talent have found that educational outcomes are much more closely related to the quality and type of students enrolled than to the school's educational policies or practices. However, yardsticks are being developed for valid comparisons of schools by partialling out such factors as family and community situations affecting outcomes. If one wants to look great as a teacher in terms of absolute achievement, all he has to do is select bright pupils. Some children seem to learn without teaching. Given half exposures and "improper sequences," there are those who show great achievement, as indicated by Elizabeth Drews:

Some boys hold the bat correctly the first time they step into the batter box and girls have been reported to mount correctly the first time they encountered a horse in the flesh (perhaps they learned from television). Music teachers both despair and rejoice over their students who can reproduce an intricate composition after one hearing, and mathematicians and scientists shake their heads over students who "intuitively leap" to right answers, spurning the step-by-step, algoristic process.[3]

Credit for achieving change in learners must be distributed in terms of teachability and the amount of relative change predicted, rather than upon an arbitrary basis of amount of change. The consideration of community and learners' characteristics in assessing effectiveness will encourage school people to undertake instructional tasks now considered hazardous although important. To bring even modest amount of change in some slow learners may represent an instructional accomplishment of the greatest order.

In saying the above, we do not want the reader to make the error of believing that behavioral change is not a function of the curriculum. It is too easy to assume that because numerous factors interact in changing behavior of a learner that curriculum leaders cannot control change or be held accountable for results. As was said earlier, if a curriculum plan brings about even 5 per cent improvement in achievement, it will be important. Perhaps the following account will illustrate how experimentation with curricular variables can lead to improved patterns of organization and more effective learning.

A certain course was 24 weeks in length. This course was rich in its variety of learning opportunities—lectures, discussions, readings, visits of resource persons, field trips, demonstrations, and extensive laboratory practice periods under competent persons. Unlike the administrators of some schools who accept the status quo of its courses, the leadership in this situation had the courage to question present practices and the genius to conceive alternative means for accomplishing instructional objectives. Instead of learners' being required to attend class sessions and to participate

[3] Elizabeth M. Drews, "Many Factors Influence Achievement and Its Assessment," *Educational Leadership*, Vol. 20, No. 1, 1962, p. 13.

in prescribed learning opportunities, it was proposed that learners be given a detailed statement of the objectives sought and descriptions of the kinds of terminal behavior to be exhibited on demand. In addition, learners were free to seek information from any source and in any order to attain the desired performance. Students were told to control their own means of instruction. Reference materials, resource persons, and other learning activities were available should the student think he needed them, but use of the opportunities was never required. Whenever a learner felt he had mastered the learning tasks, he was granted an individual interview to demonstrate his attainment of the objective. During the demonstration, he received confirmation of satisfactory attainment or correction from the teacher.

What were the results of abandoning teacher-controlled instruction in favor of specifying objectives and learner-controlled instruction? First, there was a 65 per cent reduction in teaching time. A large percentage of learners reached the criterion of achievement in six weeks; others within eight weeks in comparison with the old time of 24 weeks. Second, students were judged "better prepared" than those from previous classes under teacher direction. Those who completed the learner-controlled course also approached subsequent assignments beyond the course with "more confidence" and required less direct supervision than students from the older course. Third, there was more accurate assessment of individual capabilities as a result of the demonstrations given during interviews. Finally, students were more willing to trade information and cooperate inasmuch as they were in competition with self rather than each other.

The lessons to be gained from the above illustration are these:

1) By identifying certain variables in a program, e.g., specification of detailed statements of objectives, freedom from required assignments, and permitting these variables to be present in some situatons and not in others, noting the consequences, a school can find out what is important or unimportant in the means of instruction. Any school can take its existing program and drop out features, or possibly add new ones, and note the effects of the modifications. The identification of the variable to be manipulated

is all-important. Unless attention is given to particular details in the curriculum, one never knows what causes difficulty or enhances learning. The measures used in assessment must, of course, be sensitive enough to record changes that occur. Sometimes differences in outcome may be present as a result of modification in programs, but the measures were not sensitive enough to record them.

2) Notice that improvement of the curriculum did not occur by trying to compare something such as television versus teacher presentation of content. Such specific variables are incomparable. For instance, one never knows whether the televised presentation represents the best possible TV or whether the teacher presentation is an exemplar of teacher behavior. Instead of trying to assess the effects of variables which are not standardized, the school should take an existing program, note what it is producing, and then manipulate variables within the program. Although treatment and consequences are known only to be true for a particular program, they can suggest variables which might be of importance in improving other particular situations.

Recommendations

1) Specify what will be acceptable evidence that learners have acquired the objectives sought from instruction. How do pupils act when they have acquired the thoughts, feelings, and actions taught? In what kinds of situations would one expect pupils to reveal that they are different because of the curriculum? Do they voluntarily read more frequently than those who have not undergone the curriculum? What kinds of things do they read now that they didn't before? Questions such as these are necessary both for clarifying the meaning of instructional objectives and for determining the effectiveness of the curriculum.

2) Devise situations both in and out of school (if the objective calls for influencing behavior out of school) which will reveal whether or not the learners have acquired the behavior desired. References given at the end of this chapter will help one in his decision about how to record the learners' responses, how to judge

the appropriateness of reponses, how many and what kinds of responses are necessary in order to make sure the learners are consistent in their behavior and have not accidentally performed as desired. Suggestions are also given in these sources for getting agreement from others (impartial judges) that the objectives have been reached, for distinguishing between those who have acquired greater or less mastery of the learning sought, and for analyzing the particular strengths and deficiencies of the respondents.

3) The principle of comprehensiveness in quality control should be followed. Collect not only evidence of the behavior logically expected from the curriculum, but also note unexpected consequences. It is not enough, for instance, to show that the introduction of a new reader in the primary grades improves the ability of pupils to read from left to right and to pronounce printed words. One also will be interested in signs of the learners' anxiety, e.g., wetting, thumb sucking, and absenteeism.

4) In analyzing learners' responses to test items and situations, consider both (a) the items' relations with level of instructional objectives, e.g., recall of basic concepts, comprehension and interpretation of subject-matter taught, application of concepts; and (b) personal characteristics of the learner, e.g., mental age, prior educational experiences, and sex. Tests must reveal the mental and emotional processes of the learner sufficiently to detect points of error.

5) Errors and weaknesses detected should be used in the following ways: (a) As the basis for inferring new instructional objectives aimed at correcting learners' deficiencies. That is, new sub-objectives dealing with prerequisites should be proposed. (b) As points of reference to guide one in introducing new learning opportunities and organizational patterns. Identification of weaknesses among a particular population of learners sets the stage for speculation and hypotheses about ways the curriculum can be strengthened in order to produce the desired change.

6) Measurement of effects should be used as a means for testing hypotheses about learning opportunities and organizational patterns. It may be found, for example, that gaps in learning have

occurred because the teacher or the instructional material (textbook) has introduced too many new ideas too soon and that not enough time has been allowed for practice with each idea for the learner to master it. The manipulation of readiness activities is but one illustration of experimentation which should go on if the curriculum plan is to be improved. Perhaps the mastery of content in a short unit of instruction which clarifies terms and language to be used in subsequent instruction will contribute significantly in the overcoming of learning difficulties. The introduction of such a unit and the noting of subsequent differences in achievement is a feasible way to experiment for curriculum improvement.

7) The selection of curriculum aspects as experimental variables, e.g., particular learning opportunities, time spent on a topic, order of introducing topics and activities, kinds and frequency of responses demanded of learners, is necessary for improvement of the curriculum. The consequences of doing something different with the variable selected is an invaluable guide to curriculum change. The following variables are examples of those which can be readily manipulated within a classroom: (a) ways of introducing and conducting a film, field trip, or other learning opportunity; (b) the offering of the opportunity itself; (c) grouping of students; (d) inductive versus deductive ordering of content; (e) remedial exercises and supplementary materials; and (f) variety of materials available.

8) It is often more fruitful to experiment with a single variable within a particular course or class than to compare the effects of two or more variables in different courses or classrooms (e.g., either adding it, deleting it, or placing it at another time in the instructional sequence). Achievement that has occurred in prior classes of a particular teacher's course can be compared with the achievement which follows the manipulation of a variable by that teacher, thereby providing evidence as to the importance of the variable for that teacher, that particular subject matter, and the population of learners with which that teacher has been working and is likely to be working. This would be an example of *within*-class experimentation as opposed to *between*-class experimentation, where, say, variables like the practice of students' correcting

test papers versus teacher correction of papers are tested in several classrooms. Between-class experimentation with one or two variables is often less definitive because of multiple factors operating in a range of classrooms. Effects produced in many classrooms are due to an almost unlimited number of variables. Effects produced in a single classroom have a better chance of being directly related to the manipulation of a single variable, because the variance in a single room is more controlled than that in several classrooms.

Unlike research in basic sciences, experimentation in the classroom is more concerned with the application and adaptation of a basic principle than with the formulation of a universal principle from a number of specific instances. In the classroom we seldom try to find a generalization about an aspect of the curriculum which will hold true in all classrooms. Rather we tentatively accept a generalization about curriculum (usually derived from a principle of psychology) and try to act in accordance with it. When it does not appear to work, our attention is drawn to unique features in the particular classroom which may keep the generalization from being universally true. The discovery of unrecognized variables of significance to instructional effectiveness in a particular classroom is a great task for curriculum inquiry on the part of administrators and teachers.

Additional Readings

Bloom, Benjamin S., ed., *Taxonomy of Educational Objectives*. New York: Longmans, Green and Company, 1956.

Buros, Oscar K., ed., *The Fifth Mental Measurements Yearbook*. Highland Park, New Jersey: The Gryphon Press, 1959.

Lindquist, E. F., ed., *Educational Measurement*. Washington, D.C.: American Council on Education, 1951.

Mager, Robert F., *Preparing Objectives for Programed Instruction*. San Francisco: Fearon Publishers, 1961.

National Society for the Study of Education, 62nd Yearbook, *The Impact and Improvement of School Testing Programs*. Chicago: The University of Chicago Press, 1963.

Testing, Testing, Testing, Report of the Joint Committee on Testing, Washington, D.C.: National Education Association, 1962.

PART V. NEW VIEWS OF OLD QUESTIONS

SCHOOL CONTROVERSIES often arise in response to curriculum content and practice. The many conflicting opinions about the desirability of traditional offerings and of changes in curriculum will not be satisfactorily resolved for all, both because of fundamental philosophical differences regarding the proper role of the school in today's world and because of personal emotional problems of critics that cannot be met through rational discussion and experimental evidence. On the other hand, many questions that have caused difficulties can be resolved by providing new information, by pointing out additional considerations relative to the question, and by offering solutions which encompass several points of view, avoiding an either–or position.

VIII. Answers to Questions Affecting Curriculum Practices

What Curriculum Best Prepares for College?

BEFORE A FULL ANSWER to this question can be given one would have to know the college the pupil wanted to enter. Colleges are not alike in what they want applicants to know and be able to do. Colleges differ in the extent to which they value a learner's intellectual ability as opposed to his performance with certain subject matter. For many colleges the performance of students in particular courses of study is not as important as whether or not the applicant scores above 110 on an intelligence test (found in about 24 cases out of 100).

The curriculum taken is of less importance than the mental ability of the pupil. We have often assumed that particular subject matter is necessary to success in college because many bright people who succeed have completed work in traditional academic subject matter. However, when bright people take work in vocational subjects instead of traditional offerings, they succeed in college just as well. Therefore, we can reasonably conclude that work in vocational or academic subjects is irrelevant in comparison to the factors of intelligence.

College entrance examinations are more descriptive of the ability sought in applicants than prescriptive of curricular content to be known. These exams are directed more at general academic

133

abilities than mastery of specific information. Most colleges want evidence of the student's verbal and mathematical aptitudes. They usually offer the applicant a wide choice in such specific subjects as English, biology, mathematics, foreign language, and social studies.

Many colleges are concerned about getting too homogeneous a student body. Most admissions offices seek students who reflect a range in grades, student activities, and personal qualifications. A "touch of cussedness" may become as desirable for candidates as "well-roundedness." At present, however, one's high school grades are of first importance in considering an applicant, because grades are a good predictor of future scholastic performance.

Among the specific habits and abilities which seem to relate to admission and retention in college are these:

a. Ability to write themes and papers that exhibit an order of precision.

b. Ability to read textbooks. It is not enough to be able to read rapidly for comprehension of ideas in simple sequence. Mastery of technical vocabulary and materials demand ability to interpret cause-and-effect relations, complex spacial relations, and chronologies.

c. Ability to use several methods of study. If the learner relies only on memorization and the teacher evaluates work in terms of understanding, the student's study habit is inadequate. Other aspects with respect to study include library skills and habits of observation (e.g., recognition of major differentiations proper within each of the subjects he will study).

d. Ability to discover what the teacher wants and willingness to meet teacher expectations. This factor is related to grade-getting ability at all school levels.

What Should Be the School's Policy for Grading and Marking?

Report cards and grades are based upon observations of pupil performance. Difficulty arises when a school does not make clear what is to be observed, how often it is to be observed, and the quality of performance expected in the observations. At times, a measure of the absolute achievement in a task or course is the proper basis for assigning a grade. A teacher of a specialistic course in shorthand, for example, should give a high grade for the course only when the student demonstrates ability to take shorthand at a commonly accepted level of proficiency demanded of secretaries. At other times, the amount of relative gain in achievement made by an individual in contrast to where he started can be the basis for grading. This is especially true in classes in which the supplementary function is being met. For example, an individual in an activity class for correction of a personal physical deficiency should be graded in terms of the gain he makes in overcoming his handicap. He is not to be graded in comparison with others, but with himself.

Courses required of all, in which exploratory and integrating functions are to be served, demand that we observe the extent to which learners make an effort to learn or participate in the opportunities provided. In other words, measurement of compliance is in order when absolute mastery cannot be expected from all and when the individual does not arrive in the learning situation with a personal stake in the enterprise. If the grade is based on a comparison of gain made by competing learners, it should be kept in mind that it is often easier to show gain when one starts far from mastery of the task, provided the learner is of equal mental ability with his running mates.

In short, at the secondary school level, courses must be designated in terms of their function(s), and policy of grading practices must correspond to the function(s) of the course. At the elementary school level, in which a single teacher offers a curriculum that fulfills all functions, multiple bases for grading must be used.

A grading policy should indicate the conditions under which evidence is to be collected. When objectives call for the learner to apply knowledge in situations outside the school, then evidence must be collected outside the school. As an example, instead of the school's always giving report cards to parents, parents might well give report cards to the school. If an objective called for the child demonstrating ability and willingness to exercise good manners in social situations, parents might provide additional evidence of the child's progress toward this objective, thereby indicating the school's effectiveness.

What About Phonics?

As a target for heated controversy, phonics rivals religion and politics (e.g., the issue of fluoridated water). "Phonics" is an umbrella term meaning such things as teaching the alphabet, the sound of letters, the use of letter names, and techniques for analyzing words. Enthusiastic spokesmen for phonics differ in their methods. Some present a phonic (sound) element, ask the child to pronounce it, show the printed symbol in a short word, and then give the learner practice in sounding the element in other printed words. Others teach children to recognize a combination of one or more consonants with a vowel (blends) rather than individual letter sounds. A currently popular "phonic word" method uses materials of graded phonic complexity in which there is a constant relationship between selected visual symbols and sounds. This system seeks to overcome the weakness in phonics systems brought by irregularity in correspondence between sound and printed letters. Methods which try to meet this weakness by teaching verbal rules to govern the exceptions are generally too difficult for young learners.

Most methods associated with phonics aim at developing a word-attack skill, an ability to orally pronounce a printed word never seen before. A child who has mastered this task is not likely to look at the word "horse" and call it "pony," a frequent occurrence during instruction by methods featuring sight recognition.

One might wonder why there is so much opposition to teaching phonics when obviously its aim is important in reading achievement. The answer centers around two arguments: (a) The teaching of a tool for analysis might better follow the child's learning that printed words (sentences) carry meaning. (b) Younger children with lower mental ages have greater success in the memorization of sight words than with phonics; therefore, it is maintained, initial instruction should be with whole words and instruction in the application of phonic principles should be deferred until it is economical in terms of effort. In short, there is a difference of opinion as to *when* the teaching of phonics can be most effective, but little disagreement that the skill it seeks to develop should not be acquired at some point.

Those who recognize the complexity of the reading task reject the notion that there is a single approach to reading mastery for all learners. The ability to pronounce a printed word is only part of the task of reading; a phonics approach contributes little, for instance, to the critical prerequisite of vocabulary development, e.g., learning the meaning of words, sentences, and longer passages.

There are values in various emphases in reading: methods that feature mastery of word attack skills, the development of meaning in printed words and sentences, and individualized instruction that stresses content and purposes vital to the child. Also, clinical techniques like kinesthetic, visual, and auditory exercises and personal counselling designed to meet perceptual and emotional reading problems of individual learners contribute. These emphases can coexist inside general education. No one group or point of view should hope to capture the reading program for itself. Instead of wasting their energy in controversy, all streams should unite against their common enemy—poor teaching: (a) the inability to define what will constitute evidence of the reading behavior sought, (b) failure to analyze prerequisites to this behavior and to know where the learner stands on these hierarchies of skills, (c) insufficient attention to making the instructional experience rewarding (this means being able to state what has been rewarding to the learner in the past and to link the present reading activity with what has become a reinforcement for the learner), and (d) insufficient opportunity to practice (master) the behavior desired.

Will the "New" Mathematics Produce a Generation of Illiterates in Arithmetic?

There are many possible inferences underlying this question. The most important one is that the new curriculum in mathematics reflects the desire of some mathematicians to make mathematicians out of capable children as opposed to an older objective of equipping all children with the tools of arithmetic for application in daily life. It would be nice to know that mathematical instruction in all grades can contribute to the training of pupils in both (a) how to think logically, to make valid deductions about numbers, and (b) how to apply fundamental processes of arithmetic in their daily lives.

Schools today want learners to know mathematics as a game of explanation and inquiry as well as an applied science. The *why* must be seen as important as the *how*.

Some concern is being expressed about the precise language used in new textbooks in mathematics. The language used is that of higher "pure" mathematics, seldom found in practice. There is a belief that some present trends emphasize sophisticated treatments before learners have had sufficient practice with the elements of logical systems (e.g., teaching the number line and applying it to the concept of numbers as opposed to learning about numbers and then applying this information to the number line). In fact, there is a concern that too much emphasis upon verbal and abstract material may drive pupils away from the subject. Arithmetic is, however, abstract. It is a theory of things called numbers, relations and operations on these numbers. It uses a language all its own to build this structure. Concrete activities can be overdone, although they are necessary if the learner is to know how to observe, select, abstract, and apply in arithmetic. Whether or not the learning of, say, multiplication as a mapping process helps the child with his arithmetic skills as well as clarifying his concept of mathematics remains to be seen.

A direct answer to the question is that there will be no loss through instructional change if these newer efforts are kept in perspective to the relevant instructional objectives (application, knowledge, and attitudes). Evidence must be collected as to the effects of new programs in each of these dimensions. The consequences of any program in mathematics is to a large extent dependent upon the preparation of the teacher. As teacher education and in-service programs provide teachers who show competence in mathematics, there is a better chance of eliminating mathematical illiteracy.

Does the Study of Grammar Increase the Student's Ability to Write Better Compositions?

In other words, is there any transfer of training from the learning of grammatical principles to the art of writing?

Today the teachers of English have delineated lines of battle and argue on one of two sides. Grammar, as it is traditionally conceived, is a description of the English language derived from the same principles from which Latin is described. Historically, when it became fashionable in the Neo-classic eighteenth century to try to imbue the vernacular with the status and propriety of the classical languages, Latinized rules were imposed on English. The fact that English and Latin neither developed the same way nor shared many important characteristics was played down. However, a Latin-based English grammar has been taught to school children for the last three hundred years and represents the grammar that you probably learned. Studies have been conducted to test the premise that good Latin grammarians are good writers, but no conclusive evidence exists to support this notion.

Just when dissatisfaction with traditional grammar was gaining force, a "new" grammar was discovered, this time through the help of anthropology. Linguistic analysts used the same procedures with the English language as are applied to new languages under anthropological study. What resulted was a more accurate, simplified description of English based not on rules of what "should be" but rather on the analysis of what "is." The new grammar, called structural, descriptive, or linguistic grammar, for example, reduces the infinite number of declarative English sentences to approximately six or seven different patterns.

The question of whether linguistic analysis helps the student's writing ability cannot be answered yet. But because of the more accurate description of the language and the notation system inherent in it ("Write a pattern-five sentence" instead of "Write a sentence which includes a subject-verb-direct object and indirect object."), linguistic grammar may provide the teacher and the student with a more workable language. There is currently resistance, of course, by some engaged in the teaching of English.

They rebel against the "new" words and usurpation of what they have always known to be "right." However, other teachers welcome the linguistic movement, for it provides a new avenue to explore, after the disheartening dead-end experienced with traditional grammar. As more students are taught this descriptive grammar, research studies will attempt to demonstrate whether the increased accuracy and simplicity of the system have had any effect on the way students write.

The answer, then, to the question of relationship of grammar and writing ability is not uniformly encouraging. It appears that the traditional, Latin-based grammar has failed to do the job. However, the "new" grammar, derived by the scientific application of a phase of anthropology to English, provides some hope. And even if the linguistic approach is not found to improve writing radically, its teaching may be justified as a simple notation system and a more accurate description of the nature of the English language.[1]

Should History and Geography Replace the Social Studies?

Three demands upon the school must be considered before answering this question. First, let it be recognized that many believe that all learners should share certain historical events and information about famous personalities. They also believe that no one is educated unless his repertoire includes traditional information about places, like the names of the capitals and "————, where the nuts come from." This kind of information seldom requires a teacher. It can be obtained through films, textbooks, and television. By requiring all to pass a specified examination on myths, legends, and geographical facts and by making encyclopedias and almanacs available, schools could quickly ensure that all possessed whatever tradition demanded with respect to this kind of information.

Second, society requires that the ground rules for citizenship in a pluralistic society be known and acted upon. These rules and premises, such as the Bill of Rights, are values which often appear

[1] Appreciation is expressed to Eva Baker of UCLA for her contribution to the above discussion of the relation between grammar and composition.

to conflict with the values of particular groups and individuals. Familiarity with the rights and responsibilities of a citizen is a first step in broadening one's perspective of values from those held by the primary group (parents and close friends) to more inclusive values of the national society.

Many of the historical exemplars, myths, and legends serve as one basis for developing both understanding of the larger values and, perhaps, a predisposition to act in accordance with them. The acquisition and the ability to apply both these premises and the political skills necessary for effective citizenship in our society, however, are not likely to be obtained from mere exposure to information. Problematic social situations are required in which there is opportunity for solving problems calling for more knowledge and skills than are found in any single subject, be it history or geography. Further, these situations must offer normative (value) orientation and choices. They must deal not only with the objective facts of the problem but also with the subjective states of learners' minds, with masses of feelings. Finally, they must go beyond expression of preference and the weighing of values to a final commitment to act.

Third, if citizens are to participate in the making of wise decisions, they must know what knowledge is needed in the solving of their problems, what the relevant sources of knowledge are, and how to acquire and interpret knowledge from these sources. Without a degree of mastery in the disciplines as described in Chapter 3, it is unlikely that citizens will be able to participate effectively. The way historians and geographers arrive at and validate their interpretations and explanations is but one requirement for the wise consumer. To this end, the school must teach history and geography as separate subjects, and not only these subjects but economics and other social sciences as well.

In short, the school in its division of labor might well teach both geography and history as separate subjects (disciplines) *and* social studies (core). The school must offer instruction in the basic structure of selected social sciences or organized disciplines. This means teaching ways of inquiry and explanation into social behavior and knowledge which is not necessarily supportive of the normative ideas held in the larger society. As indicated in Chapter 5, we hold that this can best be done within the cortical curriculum. Also, through the study of social problems, the school must establish relationships among fields of knowledge (both prescriptive and descriptive knowledge, scientific as well as normative knowledge). This should occur within the nuclear social studies curriculum, as in a core program.

What Are Suggested Ways to Individualize Instruction and to Increase the Range of Educational Offerings in the Small School?

We have taken the position that the number of offerings is less important than their quality. We assume that quality depends upon the extent to which offerings have been selected in accordance with the principles stated in Chapters 3 and 5. The tendency of schools is to limit the number of subjects offered on the basis of financial costs and the educational principle of mastery. The latter includes the belief that pupils gain more intellectual control by restricting their studies to a few fields than by acquiring a smattering from various peripheral areas.

When necessary to individualize instruction through the addition of course offerings not readily available, a school should make use of correspondence courses, educational television, and programed instruction. Most state universities offer a supervised correspondence study program. Hundreds of these courses are available, primarily designed for students in regular attendance at a high school. Many of them may be applied for credit toward high school graduation and in fulfillment of requirements for entrance to a college. Correspondence courses, designed for the individual, may also be adapted to the needs of study groups. Those interested in correspondence courses should write to the department of correspondence instruction of their state university. Information regarding the availability of self-instructional programs is issued by the Superintendent of Documents, U.S. Government Printing Office, Washington, D.C., and the Center for Programed Instruction, Inc., 365 West End Avenue, New York 10024, New York.

Through televised courses, independent study, and special small-group instruction during the activity curriculum, many pupils in small schools qualify for advanced placement upon entrance to college. Advanced placement examinations are administered by the College Entrance Examination Board. These examinations are designed to assess competence in college-level courses in eleven fields. The course descriptions in this program are available from the College Entrance Examination Board.

Schools located near colleges and universities have made arrangements for pupils with special abilities to attend the college for certain courses given two to six hours a week during the semester on the college campus. In this way, high school students earn college credit and are not delayed in their normal progress, while also maintaining their status and program in the high school.

The use of community resource persons and centers of employment in supplementing the educational opportunities of selected students, such as those who are not interested in college, is recommended.

Is the Self-contained Classroom Superior to the Departmentalized?

Superior in what way? Sometimes it is argued, but inconclusively shown, that the self-contained classroom, in which pupils have contact with one teacher and association with the same group of peers for most of the school day, gives the teacher greater opportunity to know the pupil intimately. This organizational structure is presumed to develop the feeling of belonging and security believed important to young learners. Better teacher–pupil relations and acceptance of self and others have frequently been mentioned as outcomes from close association with a teacher who really cares. It is contended that the self-contained classroom is a deterrent to the fragmentation of both pupil and knowledge, inasmuch as the teacher may see the learner in a number of learning situations. Reinforcement of previous learnings and the building of relationships among fields of knowledge are thought by some to occur best in a classroom in which pupils pursue several instructional goals under the direction of one teacher.

One the other hand, academic excellence is believed speeded in the departmentalized classroom in which the teacher's major interest and preparation equip her to make a single field of knowledge systematic and meaningful to the learner. It is claimed that this pattern of organization offers economy through the efficient use of space and materials, provision for individual talents, and intensive treatment of a study. Departmentalization is said to have its own safety valve against isolated knowledge for as one goes deeply into a field, he must necessarily widen his experience in other areas. Better to place a child with some qualified teachers than with a single teacher who is not qualified in all areas in which the child is to receive instruction.

Now there is nothing in the establishment of these classroom patterns that guarantees that particular results will follow. Some teachers in self-contained classrooms often divide the day and subject into many fragmented experiences. It is a myth that all teachers in self-contained classrooms are warm and friendly. Under a single-teacher system, a child is most unfortunate when confined with a witch. In a multi-teacher system, the odds are that not all teachers will be witches. Likewise, one cannot assume that all teachers in departmentalized classrooms are highly competent in their subject matter.

Efforts to make both organizational structures more inclusive are found in (a) self-contained instruction where pupils have special instruction from experts in the arts, homemaking, science, and the like; and (b) departmentalized schools with pupil-centered homerooms as well as teams of teachers whose members possess individual specialities assuming responsibility for the instructional guidance of a single group of pupils.

Actually, the question of the best administrative organization is the shadow of the problem rather than its substance. The central questions to be raised are: What are the concepts, skills, and values to be learned? What experiences are helpful in reaching the outcomes sought? Whether self-contained or departmentalized, teachers can make good use of the organizational elements described in Chapter 4. The teacher in a departmentalized school who selects subject matter content as an element to be mastered by pupils must also consider the areas of interest by which he can help pupils grasp the desired understanding. The teacher in the self-contained classroom may take the personal concern of her pupils or a current social problem as his point of departure. If so, the key concept and intellectual tools of the subject-matter fields must be mastered before they can be used in controlling the concern or problem at hand. Logically, we may expect the self-contained pattern to be more appropriate for core and activity (nuclear) curriculum which calls for application of knowledge, and the departmentalized pattern to be more useful in disciplined (cortical) curriculum in which theoretical concepts and habits are being formulated.

Are "Life Adjustment" and "Progressive Education" Dead in Our Time?

"Life adjustment" and "progressive education" are slogans. They are poetic terms in the sense that their meaning is conveyed through the emotional tone of one's voice and the context of what is said. Each individual has his own picture of what the words mean. Thoughtful people respond to these terms by asking: "What practices does your use of these terms exclude?" and "What practices does your use of terms require?"

Even John Dewey found it necessary to say: "I am not, I hope and believe, in favor of any ends or any methods simply because the name progressive may be applied to them. The basic question concerns the nature of education with no qualifying adjectives prefixed."[2]

To Dewey, as to men through the centuries, the fundamental issue is not new versus old education but a question of what anything whatever must be to be worthy of the name Education. Originally, "progressive" was frequently associated with schools and teachers that were humane rather than harsh; with the practice of mutual consultation rather than coercion and repression. Failure to adequately interpret in school settings the ancient humanistic ideals such as self-expression made it necessary for men like Dewey to protest schoolmen who catered to caprice and who did

[2] John Dewey, *Experience and Education*. New York: The Macmillan Company, 1938, p. 115–16.

not help their charges learn to persevere in overcoming obstacles.

There is a common practice of blaming professional educators for a fairly long list of situations when things are not going as we would like them to. Better we blame our troubles on "the ornery world," not look for devils! Those who believe that modern school administrators are responsible for "life adjustment," defined as a concern for making education contribute to a workaday world, should look at history. The early Athenians offered intellectual training of the type needed for the activities of the assembly and the market place. Similar demands for utilitarianism prevailed in Ancient Rome, in the Saracenic high culture of Spain, and among European social realists of the sixteenth century. Montaigne, for example, criticized the practice of cramming the memory with facts instead of equipping one with the basis for making sensible choices and getting along efficiently with his fellows and enjoying his leisure hours. So too in the eighteenth century, our own Ben Franklin fought for a type of secondary education which would prepare for the activities of common life and not just for college.

It is false, however, to conclude that the ideal of education's being related to daily living has been continuously dominant throughout history. On the contrary, schools have maintained a zigzag course. Whenever practical education prevailed for a period of time, a theoretical type came into being to correct the abuses of the former. So it has been with other historical issues which underlie our current controversies and problems.

Shall schooling be for the benefit of society or for the benefit of the individual; for the few or for the many; for indoctrination and conformity or for original thinking; through the methods of imitation or judgment; through compulsion or interest? As noted in previous chapters of this book, we have urged that the learner, society, and the states of knowledge (theory and practice) all be taken into account to produce an inclusive curriculum. We are opposed to an either–or position.

At the moment there is a swing toward theoretical education (the disciplines) following a period in which emphasis upon practical education received more attention. Yet even before this swing toward the disciplines is in full momentum, social conditions are giving rise to demands for schooling which will make a difference in the practical actions of pupils in ethical and moral living; schooling through which youth will learn to be more effective home members, workers, and citizens.

No, the ideals of life adjustment and progressive education are not dead in this time any more than they have been throughout the ages. Our never-ending task is to determine the forms in which these ideals will find expression in the light of changed social and intellectual conditions.